Motorola Razr Plus 2025 User Guide

Step-by-Step Instructions, Tips, and
Troubleshooting for Mastering Your
Foldable Smartphone

Oksana Chalifour

Table Of Contents

5

Introduction

Welcome to the **Motorola Razr Plus 2025**, a truly revolutionary smartphone designed to offer a seamless, cutting-edge experience. With its stunning foldable display, AI-powered features, and powerful performance, the **Razr Plus 2025** is here to change the way you interact with your smartphone. Whether you're upgrading from an older device or embracing foldable technology for the first time, this user guide will walk you through everything you need to know about getting started with your device.

What Makes the Motorola Razr Plus 2025 a Game-Changer?

The **Motorola Razr Plus 2025** is not just another smartphone; it's a combination of **innovation, elegance**, and **functionality**. As part of the iconic **Motorola Razr** family, it brings back the classic flip phone design but takes it to a whole new level with a **foldable AMOLED display**. When folded, it's compact and portable, but when unfolded, it transforms into a full-size smartphone with an immersive screen. This unique combination makes it stand out in a market filled with standard smartphones.

Why Should You Be Excited About the Razr Plus 2025?

- **Foldable Technology**: The main highlight of the **Razr Plus 2025** is its **foldable screen**, offering **portability** without compromising on screen size. It combines the benefits of a pocket-friendly design with a large, immersive display that can be folded for easier carrying.

- **Camera Innovation**: With **AI-powered cameras**, the **Razr Plus 2025** ensures you can take amazing photos and videos in any lighting condition. Whether it's for daily snapshots, selfies, or professional-quality video recordings, the camera system adapts to your needs.

- **Top Performance**: The **Snapdragon 8 Gen 2** chipset provides **fast processing speeds** and **smooth multitasking**, allowing you to run demanding apps, play games, and enjoy high-speed 5G connectivity without any lag.

- **Battery Life & Charging**: Featuring a **4000mAh battery**, the **Razr Plus 2025** provides reliable battery life. With **fast charging** capabilities, you can quickly recharge the phone when you're in a pinch, ensuring you're always ready to go.

Key Features You'll Love

1. **Foldable AMOLED Screen**: Experience a sleek, modern phone that folds to fit in your pocket, yet opens up into a large, high-resolution screen for watching videos, gaming, and browsing the web.

2. **AI-Powered Camera System**: Take stunning photos with the **48MP rear camera** and **32MP front-facing camera**, powered by **AI technology** to enhance every shot, from day to night.

3. **High-Speed Performance**: Powered by **Snapdragon 8 Gen 2** and **Android 14**, your phone will run apps, games, and multitask with

ease. The **5G connectivity** ensures faster internet speeds, so you're always connected.

4. **Battery and Fast Charging**: A large **4000mAh battery** keeps your phone running all day, with **30W turbocharging** that gets you back up and running in no time.

5. **Ready For Mode**: Use your **Razr Plus 2025** as a desktop when connected to an external display, allowing you to work, present, or stream with ease.

What's Included in the Box

When you open the box, you'll find everything you need to get started with your **Motorola Razr Plus 2025**:

- **The Motorola Razr Plus 2025** smartphone itself

- **USB-C Charging Cable** for fast, efficient charging

- **Wall Adapter** for connecting to a power outlet

- **SIM Ejector Tool** to insert your SIM card

- **Quick Start Guide** to help you set up and get familiar with your device

- **Warranty Information** in case you need support or service in the future

It's important to check that all of these items are included when you first open the box so you can get started without any delays.

What to Expect During the First Few Days of Use

When you first power on the **Motorola Razr Plus 2025**, you'll be prompted to go through a few setup steps:

1. **Sign in to Your Google Account**: This will sync your contacts, calendar, and apps.

2. **Set Up Your Fingerprint or Face Unlock**: The **Razr Plus 2025** supports advanced biometric security features, so you can unlock the phone using your **fingerprint** or **facial recognition** for extra security and convenience.

3. **Customize Your Settings**: Take a few minutes to personalize your device by choosing your wallpaper, setting up your home screen, and adjusting sound and notification preferences.

4. **Install Essential Apps**: Head to the Google Play Store to download your favorite apps. You can also transfer data from your old device to your **Razr Plus 2025** if needed.

In these first few days, we recommend exploring the **foldable screen** functionality and testing the **AI camera** to understand how it adapts to different conditions. The **Razr Plus** is packed with features that may be new to you, and experimenting will help you get the most out of your device.

A Quick Look at the Foldable Design

The **foldable display** is one of the most innovative features of the **Motorola Razr Plus 2025**. Here's how the foldable technology changes the way you use your phone:

- **When Folded**: The **Razr Plus** has a small, compact form, making it easy to carry around.

With the front **quick glance display**, you can check your notifications, time, weather, or reply to a text without even opening the phone.

- **When Unfolded**: Open it up, and you'll have a full-sized screen that's great for watching movies, browsing, or gaming. The **6.9-inch AMOLED screen** is vivid, sharp, and perfect for media consumption.

The foldable nature also brings some practical benefits, such as the ability to slip the phone into tighter spaces like smaller pockets, while still giving you a large and **immersive screen** when needed.

Why the Razr Plus 2025 Is Perfect for You

Whether you're someone who loves technology or simply wants a stylish, high-performance device, the **Motorola Razr Plus 2025** delivers. It's for anyone who values **design**, **performance**, and **innovation**. If you want a smartphone that looks and feels like the future, the **Razr Plus 2025** is the ideal choice.

This is just the beginning of your journey with the **Motorola Razr Plus 2025**. In the next chapters, we'll guide you through all the essential steps, from setting up the phone to using advanced features. Stay tuned, and let's get started!

Initial Setup

Getting started with your **Motorola Razr Plus 2025** is easy when you follow the setup process step by step. This chapter will guide you through turning on your phone for the first time, connecting to Wi-Fi, activating your SIM/eSIM, signing in to your Google account, and more. Whether you're familiar with smartphones or this is your first one, we'll explain everything in detail, making it simple and clear.

Turning On the Phone for the First Time

Let's begin by turning on your phone. Here's how you do it:

1. **Find the Power Button**:

   o The **power button** is on the **right side** of your phone. It's located just below the **volume buttons**.

   o It's a small, circular button, easy to spot, and this is the button you'll use to turn the phone on and off.

2. **Turn On Your Phone**:

   o **Press and hold** the **power button** for **about 3-4 seconds**.

   o You'll feel a gentle vibration, and then the **Motorola logo** will appear on the screen. This means your phone is powering up.

3. **Wait for the Phone to Start**:

   ○ The phone will take a few moments to load the software and get ready to use. The **Motorola logo** should disappear, and you'll see a welcoming screen where you can select your **language**.

Connecting to Wi-Fi and Mobile Networks

Now that your phone is powered on, the next step is to connect to the **internet**. You can either use **Wi-Fi** or your **mobile network (SIM/eSIM)**. Here's how to do both:

Connecting to Wi-Fi

1. **Choose Your Wi-Fi Network**:

   ○ After the phone powers up and shows the welcome screen, it will ask you to connect to Wi-Fi.

   ○ A list of available **Wi-Fi networks** will appear on the screen.

   ○ Find your **Wi-Fi network name** (SSID) and **tap** on it.

2. **Enter Your Wi-Fi Password**:

   ○ Your phone will ask you to type in the **Wi-Fi password** for your home network.

   ○ Carefully type in the password using the on-screen keyboard.

- o Make sure to type **uppercase and lowercase** letters exactly as they appear in your password.

3. **Tap "Connect"**:

- o Once you've typed in the password, tap **Connect**. Your phone will attempt to connect to the network.

- o If everything is correct, you'll see a **Wi-Fi icon** at the top of your screen to show that you're connected.

Connecting to Mobile Networks (SIM or eSIM)

1. **Insert Your SIM Card (If Applicable)**:

- o If you're using a **physical SIM card**, you'll need to insert it into the phone.

- o To do this, find the **SIM tray** on the **left side** of the phone.

- o Use the **SIM ejector tool** (included in the box) to push gently into the small hole beside the SIM tray. This will pop the tray out.

- o Place the **SIM card** into the tray, ensuring it's placed correctly (with the metal part facing down).

- o Push the tray back into the phone until it clicks into place.

2. **Activate eSIM**:

o If you're using **eSIM** (digital SIM), your phone will prompt you to follow the instructions to set it up.

o Typically, you'll be asked to scan a **QR code** provided by your mobile carrier or input **activation details** manually.

3. **Check Mobile Network Connection**:

o After inserting the SIM or setting up eSIM, your phone should automatically connect to the mobile network.

o Look for the **signal bars** at the top of the screen to confirm that you're connected to your mobile network.

Inserting SIM Card / eSIM Setup

Now let's focus on ensuring your **SIM card** (or **eSIM**) is properly set up for making calls and using mobile data.

1. **Locate the SIM Tray**:

o The **SIM tray** is on the **left side** of the phone.

o Use the **SIM ejector tool** to pop the tray out by gently inserting the tool into the small hole next to the tray.

2. **Insert the SIM Card**:

o Place your **SIM card** into the tray, ensuring the card fits snugly into the tray slot.

- The **gold contacts** of the SIM should face down.

- Once the SIM card is properly inserted, carefully slide the tray back into the phone.

3. **Activate Your eSIM**:

- If you're using **eSIM** instead of a physical SIM card, follow the on-screen instructions to activate it.

- This usually involves scanning a QR code provided by your carrier or entering the activation details manually.

- Once activated, the phone will show your carrier's name in the top status bar.

Setting Up Your Google Account

Having a **Google account** is essential to use many of your phone's features, such as the **Google Play Store**, **Gmail**, and **Google Drive**. Here's how to sign in:

1. **Sign In with Your Google Account**:

- After you've connected to Wi-Fi or mobile data, your phone will ask you to sign in with your **Google account**.

- If you already have a Google account (for Gmail, YouTube, or Google services), tap on **Sign in**.

- Enter your **email address** and **password** associated with your Google account. If you don't have one, tap on **Create Account** and follow the steps to make a new one.

2. **Agree to Google's Terms and Conditions**:

   o You'll be prompted to read and agree to Google's **Terms of Service** and **Privacy Policy**. Tap **I Agree** to proceed.

3. **Choose to Enable Google Services**:

   o The phone will offer additional settings, such as location services and backup options. You can choose to enable these for better functionality.

   o If you'd like your apps, photos, and data to be backed up automatically to **Google Drive**, tap **Turn On**.

4. **Tap "Next" to Complete Google Setup**:

   o Once you've signed in, your **Google account** will sync with your phone, and you'll be ready to access Google services.

Restoring Data from Previous Devices

If you're switching from an old device, you can restore your apps, contacts, messages, and more:

1. **Restore from an Android Device**:

- After signing in to Google, the phone will ask if you'd like to restore your apps and data from a previous Android device.

- Tap **Restore** if you have a backup on Google Drive or select **Restore from an Android Device** if your old device is nearby.

- Follow the instructions to pair the devices and transfer your data.

2. **Choose Which Data to Restore**:

- You'll have the option to choose what to restore, such as apps, contacts, messages, and photos.

- Select the data you want to restore and tap **Next** to start the process. It may take a few minutes, depending on how much data needs to be transferred.

Setting Up Fingerprint and Face Unlock

For added security and convenience, you can set up **Fingerprint Unlock** and **Face Unlock**. Here's how to do it:

1. **Set Up Fingerprint Unlock**:

- When prompted, select **Fingerprint** as a security option.

- Place your **finger on the fingerprint sensor** located on the **power button** (on the side of the phone).

- Follow the on-screen instructions to scan your fingerprint. You'll be asked to lift and reposition your finger a few times to make sure it's registered correctly.

2. **Set Up Face Unlock**:

- After setting up fingerprint recognition, you'll be prompted to set up **Face Unlock**.

- The phone will use its **front camera** to scan your face and recognize it for easy unlocking.

- Hold your phone at eye level, and follow the prompts to register your face.

3. **Set a Backup Lock Screen Option**:

- After setting up fingerprint or face unlock, it's important to set a **backup lock screen method** in case the biometric options don't work.

- You can set a **PIN**, **pattern**, or **password** for this purpose. Follow the on-screen instructions to set up a backup.

Completing the Initial Setup Process

Now that your essential setup tasks are complete, let's wrap up the final steps.

1. **Final Setup Review**:

   o You'll be asked to review some additional settings, like turning on location services and deciding whether you want personalized ads from Google.

   o You can customize these settings based on your preferences.

2. **Tap "Finish"**:

   o After reviewing everything, tap **Finish** to complete the initial setup.

   o Your phone is now ready to use!

Now, your **Motorola Razr Plus 2025** is all set up and ready to go! You can start exploring your new device, downloading apps, and enjoying all the great features it has to offer. The setup process is complete, but remember, if you ever need to make changes or update settings, you can always access them through the **Settings** app at any time.

Understanding the Hardware

In this chapter, you will learn about the key hardware components of your **Motorola Razr Plus 2025**, how to interact with them, and how to care for them. We'll go through the phone's buttons, foldable screen, charging ports, and cameras, as well as provide tips for maintaining the device.

Overview of the Physical Buttons and Ports

The physical buttons and ports of your Motorola Razr Plus 2025 are essential for interacting with your phone. Let's break down their location and usage step by step.

1. Power Button (Right Side)

- **Where it is**: The **power button** is located on the **right side** of the device, just below the **volume buttons**.

- **What it does**: This button serves multiple purposes:

  o Turns the phone on and off.

  o Locks and unlocks the screen.

  o Used for **fingerprint recognition** if set up.

How to Use:

1. **To turn on the phone**: Press and **hold** the power button for about **3 seconds**. You should see the Motorola logo on the screen as it powers up.

2. **To lock the phone**: Press the power button **once**. This will lock the phone and turn off the screen.

3. **To unlock with your fingerprint**: If you've set up the fingerprint security, **place your finger** gently on the power button to unlock the phone.

2. Volume Buttons (Right Side)

- **Where it is**: The **volume buttons** are located just **above** the power button on the right side of the device.

- **What they do**: The volume buttons control the sound levels for media, calls, and notifications.

How to Use:

1. **To increase volume**: Press the **top button (+)** to increase the volume.

2. **To decrease volume**: Press the **bottom button (-)** to lower the volume.

3. **To mute your phone**: Press both volume buttons **simultaneously** to mute the phone or turn on **Do Not Disturb**.

3. SIM Tray / eSIM Slot (Left Side)

- **Where it is**: The **SIM tray** is located on the **left side** of the phone.

- **What it does**: This tray holds your physical **SIM card** or can be used for **eSIM** activation.

How to Use:

1. **To insert the SIM card**: Use the **SIM ejector tool** (included in the box). Insert it into the small hole next to the SIM tray. When the tray pops out, place your **SIM card** in the correct position and push the tray back in.

2. **To set up eSIM**: If you are using an eSIM, follow the on-screen prompts to activate it. You may need a **QR code** from your network provider to complete the activation.

4. USB-C Charging Port (Bottom Center)

- **Where it is**: The **USB-C charging port** is located at the **bottom center** of the device.

- **What it does**: The charging port is used for charging your phone and connecting external accessories.

How to Use:

1. **To charge your phone**: Plug one end of the **USB-C cable** into the charging port and connect the other end to a **wall adapter**.

2. **For data transfer**: You can also use this port to transfer files from your phone to a computer or another device by connecting the phone to a **USB cable**.

5. Speaker (Bottom Right)

- **Where it is**: The **speaker** is located just to the **right** of the USB-C charging port at the bottom of the phone.

- **What it does**: This speaker emits sound for calls, media, and notifications.

How to Use:

1. **Adjust volume**: You can adjust the speaker volume using the **volume buttons**.

2. **For better sound quality**: Turn on **Dolby Audio** in your phone's settings under **Sound** to improve the audio experience.

Foldable Screen Features and Care

The foldable screen is one of the most exciting features of the **Motorola Razr Plus 2025**, giving you the flexibility of a large screen in a compact form.

1. Foldable Screen Overview

- **What it is**: The **foldable screen** is a flexible display that allows the phone to be folded in half. When folded, the phone is compact and easy to carry. When opened, it reveals a large screen for media, browsing, and more.

How to Use:

1. **To unfold the phone**: Gently grab the top and bottom edges of the phone and pull apart. The hinge will open smoothly.

2. **To fold the phone**: Gently close the phone, making sure the two halves meet properly.

2. Screen Care Tips

Taking care of your foldable screen is important to ensure it lasts longer.

How to Care for the Screen:

1. **Clean regularly**: Use a **microfiber cloth** to gently wipe the screen. Avoid harsh chemicals, as they can damage the screen.

2. **Avoid scratches**: Keep the phone in a **protective case** or avoid placing it near sharp objects like keys, coins, or pens that could scratch the display.

3. **Don't force folding**: Always fold and unfold the phone slowly and gently. Avoid forcing it.

The Hinge Mechanism:

The **hinge** is a critical part of your phone's design, allowing it to fold and unfold smoothly.

1. Hinge Location

- **Where it is**: The **hinge** is located at the center of the phone, running vertically when the device is folded.

2. How It Works

- **What it does**: The hinge allows the screen to bend without breaking, making it flexible and durable. The mechanism ensures a smooth transition from folded to unfolded modes.

How to Use:

1. **Opening the phone**: Hold the device gently by the edges and unfold it slowly. The hinge will naturally guide the screen into place.

2. **Closing the phone**: Fold the device by gently bringing both halves together. Let the hinge close naturally.

3. Hinge Care Tips

Taking care of the hinge is just as important as caring for the screen.

How to Care for the Hinge:

1. **Keep it clean**: Periodically clean the hinge area with a microfiber cloth to remove any dust or debris.

2. **Avoid forcing the fold**: Never force the phone to fold or unfold. Let the hinge move naturally to avoid damaging the mechanism.

Charging Your Motorola Razr Plus

Proper charging habits will keep your phone's battery in good health.

1. Charging Methods

- **What it is**: The Motorola Razr Plus supports **USB-C charging** and **wireless charging**.

How to Charge Your Phone:

1. **USB-C charging**: Plug the **USB-C cable** into the charging port at the bottom of the device. Connect the other end to a compatible **wall adapter** to start charging.

2. **Wireless charging**: If you have a **Qi-compatible wireless charger**, place your phone on the charging pad to charge it without plugging in the cable.

2. Fast Charging

- **What it is**: The Razr Plus supports **fast charging** that can quickly charge your phone.

How to Enable Fast Charging:

1. Use a charger that supports **18W or higher USB-C charging**.

2. Plug it in, and your phone will charge at a faster rate.

Audio and Speaker Setup

The audio quality on your Motorola Razr Plus will enhance your media experience, and the speakers offer clear sound for calls and entertainment.

1. Dolby Audio

- **What it is**: The device supports **Dolby Audio**, which optimizes the sound output for a richer experience.

How to Use Dolby Audio:

1. **Enable Dolby Audio**: Go to **Settings** > **Sound** > **Dolby Audio** and turn it on for improved sound.

Cameras: Front and Rear Features

The Razr Plus offers both front and rear cameras for a range of photography and video needs.

1. Front Camera

- **Where it is**: The **front-facing camera** is located at the top of the screen when the phone is unfolded.

How to Use:

1. **Taking selfies**: Open the **Camera app**, and tap the **flip icon** to switch to the front camera.

2. Rear Camera

- **Where it is**: The **rear camera** is located on the back of the phone.

How to Use:

1. **Taking photos with the rear camera**: Open the **Camera app** and take photos with the rear lens. You can use the rear camera for higher-quality images compared to the front camera.

Navigating the Display: Single Screen vs. Folded Mode

The display of your phone will change depending on whether it's folded or unfolded.

1. Single Screen Mode (Unfolded)

- When the phone is fully unfolded, you get a large screen that is perfect for viewing videos, browsing, and using apps.

2. Folded Mode

- When folded, the phone becomes compact. You can view basic notifications, check the time, and interact with apps from the **external screen**.

By now, you should be comfortable navigating and interacting with the **Motorola Razr Plus 2025's hardware**. By following these simple, detailed steps, you'll be able to use your device effectively and keep it in great condition for a long time.

Customizing Your Razr Plus

One of the great things about your **Motorola Razr Plus 2025** is how much you can personalize it. From changing the way it looks to setting up shortcuts and gestures, customizing your device makes it easier to use and more fun. In this chapter, we will walk you through each step to help you make your **Razr Plus** truly yours.

Customizing the Home Screen

The home screen is where you interact with your phone the most, so making it easy to navigate is important. Luckily, customizing the home screen is simple and fun!

Moving App Icons Around

- **What is it?** You can rearrange the app icons to suit your needs. Whether you want to move your most-used apps to the front or organize them in a way that makes sense to you, it's quick and easy.

How to Move App Icons:

1. **Tap and hold** any app icon on your home screen for about one second.

2. The app will lift up, and you'll see a grid of available spaces on your screen.

3. **Drag** the app to the spot where you want it to appear.

4. Once you're happy with the new position, **release** the app. It's that simple!

Example: If you use your email app every day, you might want to move it to the top of the home screen for quick access.

Creating Folders

- **What is it?** Folders allow you to group similar apps together—like having a folder for all your social media apps or your music apps.

How to Create a Folder:

1. Tap and hold an app icon that you want to place in a folder.

2. **Drag it** onto another app that you want to group it with.

3. The apps will now combine into a folder. You can **rename** the folder by tapping on the name and typing something that makes sense, like "Social" or "Games."

4. To add more apps to the folder, just drag them into the same folder.

Setting Wallpapers and Themes

Changing your wallpaper and theme helps give your phone a personal touch. Whether you prefer a sleek, minimalistic look or something vibrant and colorful, customizing your wallpaper and theme can match your style.

Changing the Wallpaper

- **What is it?** Wallpaper is the background image that appears on your home screen and lock screen.

How to Change the Wallpaper:

1. Tap and hold on an empty space on your home screen.

2. A menu will pop up—tap **Wallpaper**.

3. You'll see two options: **Home Screen** or **Lock Screen**. Choose which one you want to change.

4. Pick an image from the default options, or tap on **Gallery** to choose an image from your own photos.

5. Adjust the image by dragging or zooming to make sure it fits the screen.

6. Press **Set Wallpaper** to apply.

Pro Tip: If you like change, you can set different wallpapers for your home screen and lock screen!

Applying a Theme

- **What is it?** Themes change the overall appearance of your phone, including icons, colors, and system UI (like the navigation bar and notification menu).

How to Apply a Theme:

1. Open **Settings** on your phone.

2. Scroll down to **Display**.

3. Tap **Theme**.

4. Choose between the **Light** or **Dark** theme based on your preference.

5. If you want to explore more theme options, you can find them in the **Google Play Store** or from Motorola's collection of themes.

Why Use Dark Mode?: Dark mode is great for saving battery life and reducing eye strain, especially in low-light environments.

Using Widgets to Personalize Your Display

Widgets are small tools that show you real-time information right on your home screen—such as weather updates, news, or music controls. They're super useful for getting quick info without opening apps.

Adding a Widget

- **What is it?** Widgets are like mini-apps that give you at-a-glance information.

How to Add a Widget:

1. **Tap and hold** an empty space on your home screen.

2. Select **Widgets** from the menu.

3. Scroll through the available widgets and tap on the one you want to add (for example, weather, calendar, or clock).

4. **Tap and hold** the widget, then **drag** it to the desired location on your home screen.

5. Release the widget to place it.

Resizing Widgets

- **What is it?** Some widgets can be resized to make them larger or smaller, depending on how much information you want displayed.

How to Resize a Widget:

1. **Tap and hold** the widget you've just placed.

2. You will see small dots or handles around the widget.

3. **Drag** the handles to resize the widget.

4. Release it when you're satisfied with the size.

Example: If you have a weather widget, you can make it bigger to show the forecast for the week or keep it small for just today's forecast.

Managing Apps: Installing, Uninstalling, and Organizing

Managing your apps is essential to keeping your device neat and running smoothly. Whether you're adding new apps, removing old ones, or organizing them, this section will help you stay organized.

Installing Apps

- **What is it?** Installing apps allows you to expand the capabilities of your phone. The Google Play Store is where you'll find apps for nearly everything.

How to Install Apps:

1. Open the **Google Play Store**.

2. Type the name of the app you want in the search bar.

3. Tap on the app from the search results.

4. Tap **Install**, and the app will automatically download and install.

5. Once installed, the app will appear on your home screen.

Example: Want to install Instagram? Just search for it, tap **Install**, and you're ready to go!

Uninstalling Apps

- **What is it?** Uninstalling apps you no longer use frees up space and keeps your phone fast.

How to Uninstall Apps:

1. **Tap and hold** the app you want to remove.

2. From the menu that appears, tap **Uninstall**.

3. Confirm by tapping **OK**, and the app will be removed from your phone.

Organizing Apps into Folders

- **What is it?** Folders help you organize your apps by category, making it easier to find them.

How to Create a Folder:

1. **Tap and hold** an app icon.

2. Drag it over another app that you want to group it with.

3. The apps will merge into a folder, and you can **rename** it for easy identification.

Adjusting Display Settings (Brightness, Night Light, etc.)

Tweaking display settings makes a huge difference in how comfortable your phone is to use, especially under different lighting conditions.

Adjusting Brightness

- **What is it?** Brightness settings control how light or dark your screen is, which can help with visibility and battery life.

How to Adjust Brightness:

1. Swipe down from the top of the screen to open the **Quick Settings** menu.

2. **Drag the brightness slider** left or right to adjust the brightness.

Enabling Night Light

- **What is it?** Night Light reduces blue light to make your screen easier on your eyes during nighttime or low-light conditions.

How to Enable Night Light:

1. Go to **Settings** > **Display** > **Night Light**.

2. Toggle **Night Light** on.

3. You can also schedule it to automatically turn on at specific times.

Theme and Font Customization

Personalizing your theme and font style can make your phone look unique to you.

Changing Font Style

- **What is it?** Changing the font style alters how text appears throughout your phone's interface.

How to Change Font Style:

1. Go to **Settings** > **Display** > **Font Size and Style**.

2. Select the font style you prefer.

Dark Mode and Accessibility Themes

Dark mode is easier on your eyes in the dark, and accessibility features help those who may need additional support when using their phone.

Enabling Dark Mode

How to Enable Dark Mode:

1. Go to **Settings** > **Display** > **Theme**.

2. Select **Dark** to enable Dark Mode, which uses darker colors for most system elements.

Moto Actions: Customizing Gestures

Moto Actions make your life easier with simple gestures.

Using Moto Actions

How to Use Moto Actions:

1. Go to **Settings** > **Moto** > **Moto Actions**.

2. Choose gestures like **Twist for Camera, Chop for Flashlight**, and **Pick up to silence** to make your device more intuitive.

Moto Display: Quick Access Features

Moto Display shows notifications, time, and other information without unlocking your phone.

Enabling Moto Display

How to Enable Moto Display:

1. Go to **Settings** > **Moto** > **Moto Display**.

2. Turn it on to see your notifications pop up on the lock screen without unlocking your phone.

Your **Motorola Razr Plus 2025** is now fully personalized! You've made your home screen uniquely yours, chosen a theme and wallpaper, organized your apps, and set up Moto Actions. Customizing your phone doesn't just make it look great—it makes it easier to use and more suited to your lifestyle. Enjoy exploring all the ways you can make your phone your own!

Navigating Android 14 Features

Android 14 introduces many new and exciting features that enhance the functionality of your Motorola Razr Plus 2025. Whether you're looking for privacy improvements, multitasking options, or customizing your phone to fit your needs, this chapter covers everything you need to know. We'll guide you through Android 14's key features step-by-step to make sure you get the most out of your device.

Exploring Android 14's New Features

Android 14 brings a range of new features designed to improve your phone's performance and make it easier to use. Here's a closer look at some of the highlights:

Personalized Lock Screen

- **What is it?** Android 14 allows you to fully personalize your lock screen with widgets, clocks, and wallpaper options. This makes your device more visually appealing and functional.

How to Customize Your Lock Screen:

1. Open **Settings** and go to **Display**.

2. Tap **Lock Screen**.

3. Here, you can change the wallpaper, choose from different clock styles, and even add widgets like weather or calendar reminders.

Improved Notifications

- **What is it?** With Android 14, notifications have been made smarter. You'll be able to group similar notifications together for easier management, and there's a better layout for notifications so you can act on them faster.

How to Manage Notifications:

1. Swipe down from the top of your screen to open the **Notification Panel**.

2. To interact with a notification, tap it. If it's an app notification, you may be able to respond directly from the panel without opening the app.

3. You can swipe notifications left or right to dismiss them or tap the three dots on the right to adjust settings for that notification.

Battery Life Enhancements

- **What is it?** Android 14 introduces smarter battery management, helping extend battery life by automatically managing app background activities.

How to Check Battery Usage:

1. Open **Settings** and go to **Battery**.

2. Here, you can see how much battery is left, which apps are consuming the most power, and whether you need to enable **Battery Saver** mode.

Privacy and Security Enhancements in Android 14

Android 14 focuses heavily on privacy and security. Here's what you need to know to keep your personal information safe:

Privacy Dashboard

- **What is it?** The Privacy Dashboard lets you see which apps are accessing sensitive data like your location, camera, or microphone.

How to Access the Privacy Dashboard:

1. Go to **Settings > Privacy**.

2. Tap on **Privacy Dashboard** to see a list of apps that have accessed your personal data over the past 24 hours.

App Permissions

- **What is it?** Android 14 gives you more control over which apps can access specific features like your location, camera, and microphone.

How to Manage App Permissions:

1. Open **Settings** and go to **Apps**.

2. Tap on **Permissions** to see which permissions each app has.

3. Tap on any app to change its permission settings. For example, if you don't want an app to access your location, you can turn off the location permission here.

Lock Screen Security

- **What is it?** You can now protect your notifications with added security, so private information isn't exposed when your phone is locked.

How to Lock Notifications on the Lock Screen:

1. Go to **Settings** > **Lock Screen**.

2. Under **Notifications**, select **Don't Show Notifications** or **Show Sensitive Content Only After Unlocking**.

How to Use Android 14 Multitasking Features

Multitasking on Android 14 is smoother than ever. With the Motorola Razr Plus 2025's foldable display, you can take advantage of these features to improve your workflow.

Split-Screen Mode

- **What is it?** Split-Screen allows you to run two apps side by side, perfect for multitasking. For example, you can browse the web while watching a video.

How to Enable Split-Screen Mode:

1. Open the first app you want to use.

2. Tap the **Recent Apps** button (the square icon at the bottom).

3. Swipe up to find the second app you want to use.

4. Tap the app's icon at the top of its preview, and select **Split-Screen**.

5. Drag the divider to adjust how much space each app takes up.

Floating Apps

- **What is it?** Floating apps are apps that open in small, movable windows on your screen, allowing you to interact with other apps while using them.

How to Use Floating Apps:

1. Open the app you want to use in floating mode.

2. Tap the **Recent Apps** button and choose the app you want to float.

3. Tap the app's icon at the top and select **Open in a Floating Window**.

Managing App Permissions in Android 14

Android 14 gives you granular control over app permissions, allowing you to customize exactly what apps can and can't do with your data.

Granting or Revoking Permissions

- **What is it?** This feature allows you to manage what permissions apps have, such as location, camera, microphone, and more.

How to Adjust App Permissions:

1. Open **Settings** > **Apps**.

2. Tap **See All Apps** and select the app you want to manage.

3. Tap **Permissions**.

4. You'll see all the permissions the app has. To change any permission, toggle the switch next to the feature (like **Location**, **Camera**, or **Microphone**).

Permission History

- **What is it?** Android 14 now tracks how often apps use sensitive features like your location or camera.

How to Check Permission History:

1. Go to **Settings** > **Privacy**.

2. Tap **Permission Manager** to see which apps have recently accessed sensitive information.

Understanding Android 14 Widgets

Android 14 makes widgets even more powerful, allowing you to interact with your favorite apps directly from the home screen.

Adding Widgets to the Home Screen

- **What is it?** Widgets display useful information right on your home screen, such as the weather, calendar, or music controls.

How to Add a Widget:

1. Tap and hold an empty space on your home screen.

2. Select **Widgets** from the menu.

3. Browse through available widgets and choose one you want.

4. Tap and hold the widget, then drag it to your desired spot on the home screen.

5. Release to place the widget.

Resizing Widgets

- **What is it?** Some widgets can be resized to take up more or less space on your home screen.

How to Resize a Widget:

1. Tap and hold the widget you want to resize.

2. Drag the corners to resize the widget.

3. Release once you have the desired size.

Customizing the Quick Settings Menu

The Quick Settings menu provides quick access to essential settings like Wi-Fi, Bluetooth, and Do Not Disturb. With Android 14, you can now customize this menu to suit your preferences.

How to Customize the Quick Settings Menu

- **What is it?** You can add or remove tiles from the Quick Settings menu to make sure you only see the settings you use the most.

How to Customize Quick Settings:

1. Swipe down from the top of the screen to open the **Quick Settings** menu.

2. Tap the **Edit** button (it looks like a pencil).

3. From here, you can drag tiles to rearrange them or tap the + sign to add new tiles for features like **Dark Mode, Battery Saver,** or **Screen Recorder**.

4. To remove a tile, simply drag it to the **Remove** area at the top.

Android 14 brings a wealth of new features to your Motorola Razr Plus 2025, allowing you to take full advantage of your device's hardware and software. From multitasking features to privacy settings and customizable widgets, Android 14 enhances your experience and makes your phone even more powerful. By exploring these features and making them your own, you'll be able to tailor your Razr Plus to meet your needs and preferences. Enjoy the journey of personalizing your phone and exploring all the possibilities Android 14 has to offer!

Motorola-Specific Features

Motorola offers several unique features on the **Motorola Razr Plus 2025** that enhance your user experience, making it not just a phone but a tool that adapts to your needs. Below, we'll explain in detail how to use each of these features to their full potential.

Moto Voice: Hands-Free Control

Moto Voice allows you to control your Motorola Razr Plus 2025 hands-free, using just your voice. It's perfect for when you're driving, cooking, or in situations where you can't physically touch the phone.

Setting Up Moto Voice:

1. **Enable Moto Voice:**

   o   Open the **Settings** app on your phone.

   o   Scroll down and tap on **Moto**.

   o   Tap on **Moto Voice** and toggle the feature to **On**.

2. **Set Up Voice Recognition:**

   o   When you enable **Moto Voice**, you'll need to set up voice recognition.

   o   Follow the instructions on your screen and say a few words or sentences as prompted. This helps Moto Voice recognize your voice specifically.

Using Moto Voice:

Once setup is complete, you can activate Moto Voice by saying **"Hey Moto"**. You can then give commands such as:

- **"Hey Moto, call Sarah"** – Initiates a call to Sarah from your contacts.

- **"Hey Moto, set an alarm for 7 AM"** – Sets an alarm.

- **"Hey Moto, open the camera"** – Opens the camera app directly.

- **"Hey Moto, turn on flashlight"** – Activates the flashlight without touching the phone.

Tips:

- **Use it when hands are full:** Moto Voice is perfect for when you need to operate your phone without touching it.

- **Maximize its potential:** You can use it for more than just basic tasks. Ask about weather, set reminders, or even control apps.

Moto Actions: Navigating with Gestures

Moto Actions are gestures that allow you to navigate and control your phone without using buttons or on-screen touches. It's a simple way to make your phone experience faster and more efficient.

Setting Up and Using Moto Actions:

1. **Enable Moto Actions:**

- Go to **Settings** > **System** > **Gestures**.

- Toggle the switch to **On** for the gestures you want to use.

2. **Popular Moto Actions and How to Use Them:**

- **Twist to Capture Photos:**

  - Twist your wrist twice (like turning a doorknob) to quickly open the camera app.

  - You can start taking pictures or videos without unlocking the phone.

- **Chop Twice for Flashlight:**

  - Make two quick downward chop motions with your hand near the phone.

  - The flashlight will turn on automatically.

- **Flip to Mute:**

  - When a call is incoming, simply flip your phone over to mute the ringer.

- **Swipe Down for Screenshot:**

  - Swipe three fingers downward on the screen to take a screenshot of what's currently displayed.

Tips for Moto Actions:

- **Use gestures frequently:** These can speed up your tasks. For example, use **Twist to Capture** for quick photos while on the go.

- **Practice the gestures:** Some of the gestures require a bit of practice, so keep trying them to get comfortable with the motions.

Moto Display: Always-On Screen Tips

Moto Display is an always-on feature that shows notifications, time, and important updates without unlocking the phone. It's useful for quickly checking important alerts without having to wake up your device.

Activating and Using Moto Display:

1. **Enable Moto Display:**

   o Open **Settings** > **Display**.

   o Scroll down and toggle the switch for **Moto Display** to **On**.

2. **How Moto Display Works:**

   o When you receive notifications (like messages or calls), they will appear on the screen, even when your phone is locked.

   o To interact with a notification, tap it to open the relevant app, or swipe it away to dismiss it.

3. **Customizing Moto Display:**

   o In the **Settings** > **Display** section, you can tweak how Moto Display works, such as adjusting the amount of time notifications stay on the screen.

Tips for Moto Display:

- **Minimal Disruption:** Moto Display gives you just the right amount of information without unlocking your phone, which is perfect for checking messages or time during meetings or classes.

- **Battery Friendly:** Moto Display is designed to be energy-efficient. However, if you want to extend battery life, you can disable it.

Ready For: Using Your Phone as a Desktop

With **Ready For**, you can use your Motorola Razr Plus 2025 as a desktop computer by connecting it to a larger display, such as a TV or monitor.

Setting Up Ready For Mode:

1. **Using a USB-C to HDMI Cable:**

   o Plug one end of the **USB-C to HDMI** cable into your Motorola Razr Plus and the other end into the HDMI port on your TV or monitor.

2. **Activating Ready For Mode:**

   o Once connected, your phone will prompt you to **Start Ready For**. Tap **Start** to initiate the desktop experience.

3. **Using Your Phone as a Desktop:**

   o Your phone's screen will transform into a desktop-like interface with resizable windows for apps, a taskbar, and a mouse and keyboard for easier navigation.

o If you have a Bluetooth keyboard and mouse, connect them to your phone to fully emulate a desktop.

Tips for Ready For:

- **Productivity:** Ready For is great for productivity, such as editing documents or giving presentations. Simply connect a Bluetooth keyboard and mouse.

- **Entertainment:** Watch movies or play games on a bigger screen with the phone as your media player.

Integrating Motorola Smart Accessories

Motorola has a range of **smart accessories** that can enhance your experience, like wireless earbuds, smartwatches, and other connected devices.

Pairing Accessories with Your Motorola Razr Plus:

1. **Pairing Bluetooth Accessories:**

   o Open **Settings** > **Bluetooth**.

   o Ensure that Bluetooth is turned on, then tap on the accessory you want to pair (e.g., a Bluetooth headset or a Moto smartwatch).

   o Follow the on-screen instructions to complete the pairing process.

2. **Using Moto Mods (If Available):**

   o Some Motorola phones allow you to attach physical Moto Mods (extra battery, speakers, etc.) to your device. Simply align the mod with the back of your phone, and it will automatically connect.

Tips for Using Motorola Accessories:

- **Keep accessories updated:** Make sure your Bluetooth devices and Moto Mods are regularly updated to avoid issues with compatibility.

- **Extra Battery Mods:** If you have a Moto Mod battery pack, attach it when you're running low on power to get extra charge.

Motorola Software Updates and Security Patches

Keeping your device up to date ensures you have the latest features, security patches, and improvements.

Checking for Updates:

1. **Automatic Updates:**

   o Go to **Settings** > **System** > **Software Updates**.

   o The phone will check automatically for updates. If available, it will prompt you to install.

2. **Manual Updates:**

o If you prefer to manually check, tap **Check for Updates** in the **Software Updates** section.

Tips for Updates:

- **Wi-Fi Connection:** It's always best to download software updates over Wi-Fi to avoid using up your mobile data.

- **Battery Life:** Make sure your phone is charged or plugged in while performing an update to prevent any interruptions.

Using AI Features on Your Motorola Razr Plus

Motorola Razr Plus 2025 comes with **AI (Artificial Intelligence)** features that optimize your phone's performance and enhance the camera's capabilities.

How AI Enhances Your Experience:

1. **Battery Optimization:**

   o AI monitors your usage and helps manage background apps, conserving battery life.

2. **Performance Enhancements:**

   o AI optimizes the phone's performance by prioritizing frequently used apps, ensuring smoother operation.

3. **AI Camera Features:**

o The camera uses AI to automatically adjust settings like exposure, focus, and white balance, giving you better photos without manual adjustments.

Tips for Using AI:

- **AI Battery Saving:** Let AI learn your phone habits so it can optimize battery usage effectively.

- **AI Camera:** Enjoy great photos effortlessly with the smart AI camera that detects scenes and adjusts automatically.

AI Camera Features:

The **AI-powered camera** on the Motorola Razr Plus 2025 is capable of delivering stunning photos with minimal effort from you. Thanks to **Smart Capture** and **Object Detection**, you can capture beautiful moments with ease.

Using AI Camera Features:

1. **Smart Capture:**

   o Open the camera app and point it at the subject.

   o The camera will automatically adjust settings based on what it detects— whether it's a person, pet, or scenery.

2. **Object Detection:**

   o The AI camera recognizes objects in your view and adjusts the focus accordingly. This ensures that the most important part of your shot is always sharp.

Tips for AI Camera:

- **Hands-Off Photography:** Let the camera do the hard work for you! Smart Capture will help make your photos look amazing.

- **Object Detection:** Capture dynamic and detailed photos with the AI's object recognition for better shots.

The **Motorola Razr Plus 2025** offers a wide variety of Motorola-specific features that make it more than just a phone. From the hands-free convenience of **Moto Voice** to the desktop-like experience with **Ready For**, you have the tools to make the most of your device. Additionally, the **AI-powered camera** and **Moto Actions** ensure that your phone adapts to your lifestyle and needs.

By exploring and using these features, you'll gain a deeper understanding of what your Motorola Razr Plus can do, making your smartphone experience truly unique and enjoyable.

Everyday Use & Features

The **Motorola Razr Plus 2025** is designed to be user-friendly for everyday tasks. From making calls and sending messages to managing photos, music, and using the foldable screen for multitasking, this chapter will guide you through the most common features and tasks on your phone.

Making and Receiving Calls

Making and receiving calls on your Motorola Razr Plus is straightforward. Here's how to use the phone's dialer:

Making a Call:

1. **Open the Phone App:**

   o From the home screen, tap the **Phone** icon. It's the green icon that looks like a handset.

2. **Dial the Number:**

   o Tap the **dialpad** (numbers) at the bottom of the screen.

   o Use the dialpad to enter the phone number you wish to call. You can also tap on the **contacts** tab if the number is saved in your address book.

3. **Make the Call:**

   o Once you've entered the phone number, tap the **green call button** (it looks like a phone receiver) to initiate the call.

Receiving a Call:

1. **Answer the Call:**

   o   When a call comes in, the screen will display the caller's information (name or number).

   o   Swipe the **green receiver** icon up to answer the call.

2. **Rejecting the Call:**

   o   If you want to decline the call, swipe the **red receiver** icon down to reject it.

Sending and Receiving Texts & Emails

Sending a Text Message:

1. **Open the Messages App:**

   o   Tap the **Messages** app (it looks like a speech bubble) on your home screen.

2. **Compose a New Message:**

   o   Tap the + icon (or the **new message** button) at the bottom right of the screen.

3. **Enter the Recipient's Name or Number:**

   o   In the **To** field, type the contact's name or phone number. If it's saved in your contacts, you can just start typing the name and select the contact.

4. **Type Your Message:**

- o   Tap the text input field and type your message using the on-screen keyboard.

5. **Send the Message:**

- o   Once you've finished typing, tap the **send button** (it looks like an arrow) to send your message.

Receiving Text Messages:

- New messages will appear in your **Messages** app.

- If you have **Moto Display** enabled, you'll see notifications on your locked screen.

- Tap on a message to open it and reply if needed.

Sending an Email:

1. **Open the Gmail App:**

- o   Tap the **Gmail** app icon (it's the red and white icon) on your home screen.

2. **Compose a New Email:**

- o   Tap the **compose button** (it looks like a pencil in a box) in the bottom-right corner.

3. **Enter the Recipient's Email:**

- o   Type the email address of the person you want to send an email to in the **To** field.

4. **Type Your Message:**

- o   Enter the subject and the content of your email.

5. **Send the Email:**

   o Once you're done, tap the **send button** (it's a paper airplane icon) at the top right.

Using Google Assistant and Voice Commands

Google Assistant is a helpful tool for hands-free interaction with your Motorola Razr Plus.

Activating Google Assistant:

1. **Using Voice Command:**

   o Simply say **"Hey Google"** to activate the Google Assistant. If voice activation isn't working, follow the steps below to enable it.

2. **Enable Voice Activation:**

   o Go to **Settings** > **Google** > **Search, Assistant & Voice** > **Google Assistant**.

   o Ensure **"Hey Google"** is enabled.

3. **Using Google Assistant:**

   o After activating Google Assistant, ask it to do things such as:

     ▪ "What's the weather like today?"

     ▪ "Set a reminder for 5 PM"

     ▪ "Play music by [artist name]"

4. **Typing Commands:**

   o You can also type your request in the **Google Assistant** window.

Using Google Assistant for Multitasking:

- Ask Google to perform tasks while you're doing something else. For example, ask **"Hey Google, send a message to John"** while browsing through apps.

Connecting Bluetooth Devices

Connecting Bluetooth devices such as wireless headphones or speakers is easy on the Motorola Razr Plus.

Pairing a Bluetooth Device:

1. **Open Bluetooth Settings:**

   o Swipe down from the top of the screen to open the **Quick Settings menu**.

   o Tap on the **Bluetooth icon** to open the Bluetooth settings, or go to **Settings** > **Connected Devices** > **Bluetooth**.

2. **Enable Bluetooth:**

   o Make sure Bluetooth is turned **on**. You should see the toggle switch turn blue.

3. **Pair a New Device:**

   o Tap **Pair new device** and make sure your Bluetooth device is in pairing mode.

o   Select your Bluetooth device from the list of available devices that appear on your phone screen.

4. **Complete the Pairing:**

o   Follow the on-screen instructions to complete the pairing process. Once paired, the device will show up under **Paired devices**.

Using the Foldable Screen for Multitasking

The **Motorola Razr Plus** has a foldable screen, allowing you to use it in multiple ways. Here's how to make the most of multitasking with your foldable screen.

Using Split Screen Mode:

1. **Open Apps:**

o   Open the apps you want to use simultaneously.

2. **Activate Split Screen:**

o   Swipe up from the bottom to see the recent apps list.

o   Tap the **app icon** of the first app you want to use and select **Split screen**.

o   Select the second app from the recent apps list to open it in the second window.

3. **Adjust Screen Size:**

o   You can adjust the size of each app by dragging the divider line in the middle of the screen.

Using Apps on the Outer Screen:

- The outer screen can be used for quick access to apps without fully unfolding the phone.

Playing Music and Videos on Your Razr Plus

Enjoy music, videos, and other media on your **Motorola Razr Plus** with ease.

Playing Music:

1. **Open the Music App:**

   o   Open the **YouTube Music**, **Spotify**, or any other music app you use.

2. **Select Your Playlist or Song:**

   o   Browse or search for the music you want to play.

3. **Adjust Volume:**

   o   Use the physical volume buttons on the side of your phone or swipe down from the top of the screen to adjust the volume.

Watching Videos:

1. **Open Your Video App:**

   o   Open an app like **YouTube**, **Netflix**, or **VLC**.

2. **Choose a Video:**

   o Tap on the video you want to watch.

3. **Using the Foldable Screen:**

   o Unfold the screen to watch the video in full size, or use the outer screen for smaller video watching when the phone is folded.

Taking Photos and Videos with the Motorola Razr Plus

The camera on the **Motorola Razr Plus** is packed with features to help you take great photos and videos.

Taking a Photo:

1. **Open the Camera App:**

   o Tap the **Camera** app on your home screen.

2. **Select Photo Mode:**

   o The default mode is **Photo**. If not, swipe through the modes to select it.

3. **Tap to Capture:**

   o Frame your subject and tap the **shutter button** (the large circle) to take the photo.

Recording a Video:

1. **Switch to Video Mode:**

o   Swipe through the modes at the top of the camera screen until you find **Video**.

2. **Record:**

o   Tap the **red record button** to start recording.

3. **Stop Recording:**

o   Tap the **stop button** (the square) when you're finished.

Editing and Sharing Photos and Videos

Once you've taken your photos or videos, you can easily edit and share them.

Editing Photos:

1. **Open the Photo:**

o   Tap on the photo you want to edit from the **Gallery**.

2. **Tap Edit:**

o   Tap the **Edit** icon (it looks like a pencil).

3. **Adjust the Photo:**

o   Use the **filters, crop, rotate,** or other editing tools to make adjustments.

4. **Save Changes:**

o   Once you're happy with your edits, tap **Save**.

Sharing Photos and Videos:

1. **Open the Photo or Video:**

   o Open the photo or video you want to share in the **Gallery**.

2. **Tap Share:**

   o Tap the **share icon** (it looks like three connected dots) and select your preferred sharing method (e.g., **Messenger, WhatsApp, Email**).

Using the Camera's AI Features for Better Shots

The **Motorola Razr Plus 2025** uses **AI features** to enhance the quality of your photos.

How AI Enhances Photos:

1. **Smart Capture:**

   o The camera will automatically adjust settings like exposure, focus, and scene detection based on what it sees in the frame (e.g., faces, landscapes).

2. **Object Detection:**

   o AI recognizes objects and optimizes the camera settings for better focus and clarity.

3. **Low Light Mode:**

o AI can enhance photos in low-light situations by adjusting the exposure and brightness for clearer shots.

Using the Razr Plus for Productivity (Document Editing, Google Workspace)

Your Motorola Razr Plus can also be used for productivity tasks.

Editing Documents:

1. **Open Google Docs:**

   o Open the **Google Docs** app or visit **docs.google.com**.

2. **Create or Edit a Document:**

   o Tap the + to create a new document or select an existing one to edit.

3. **Save Changes:**

   o Your document will automatically save in **Google Drive**, but you can tap the **back button** to ensure it's saved.

By following these steps, you can make the most of your **Motorola Razr Plus 2025**, whether you're making calls, sending messages, using Google Assistant, managing media, or multitasking with the foldable screen. Enjoy your device and the seamless experience it offers!

Security and Privacy

Your **Motorola Razr Plus 2025** comes with a range of security and privacy features that help protect your personal information. This chapter will walk you through how to secure your phone with PINs, passwords, fingerprint, Face Unlock, and other security tools. You'll also learn how to manage your data and app permissions, set up two-factor authentication (2FA), and use VPNs and encryption for better privacy.

Lock Screen Security Options: PIN, Pattern, Password

Securing your phone starts with setting up a **lock screen**. A lock screen prevents unauthorized access to your phone. Here's how you can set it up:

Setting a PIN, Pattern, or Password:

1. **Open Settings:**

   o From the home screen, swipe up to open the **Apps** menu and tap on **Settings**.

2. **Navigate to Security Settings:**

   o Scroll down and tap on **Security**. This section allows you to set up all the security options for your phone.

3. **Choose Screen Lock Method:**

   o Tap on **Screen lock**.

   o Here, you will be given several options:

- **PIN**: A 4-6 digit number that you need to enter to unlock your phone.

- **Pattern**: A pattern made by connecting dots in a grid.

- **Password**: A combination of letters, numbers, and symbols for a stronger security option.

4. **Set Your Preferred Option:**

   o Choose your preferred lock screen method and follow the on-screen instructions to set it up.

5. **Confirm Your Lock Method:**

   o Depending on your choice, you may need to re-enter the PIN, pattern, or password to confirm it.

6. **Additional Lock Screen Options:**

   o You can choose to show or hide notifications on the lock screen or configure other security options like **Smart Lock**.

Enabling Fingerprint and Face Unlock

For faster and more convenient security, you can use your **fingerprint** or **Face Unlock**. This allows you to unlock your device with just your fingerprint or by scanning your face.

Setting Up Fingerprint Unlock:

1. **Open Settings:**

   o Go to **Settings** > **Security** > **Fingerprint**.

2. **Add Fingerprint:**

   o Tap **Add fingerprint**.

   o Follow the on-screen instructions to place your finger on the fingerprint sensor multiple times. Make sure to lift and place your finger in different positions each time for accurate scanning.

3. **Set Backup Screen Lock:**

   o You'll be asked to set a backup screen lock (PIN, pattern, or password) in case the fingerprint scanner doesn't work.

4. **Enable Fingerprint for Unlocking:**

   o Once set up, you can use your fingerprint to unlock the phone, confirm purchases, or authorize apps.

Setting Up Face Unlock:

1. **Open Settings:**

   o Go to **Settings** > **Security** > **Face Unlock**.

2. **Add Face Data:**

- Tap **Add face data** and follow the instructions to set up **Face Unlock**. Position your face in front of the front-facing camera, and it will scan your face for recognition.

3. **Enable Face Unlock for Security:**

   - After setup, you can unlock your phone just by looking at it.

Setting Up Two-Factor Authentication (2FA)

Two-Factor Authentication (2FA) adds an extra layer of security to your accounts, such as your Google or email account. This ensures that even if someone knows your password, they can't access your account without the second factor.

Setting Up 2FA for Google Account:

1. **Open Settings:**

   - Go to **Settings** > **Google** > **Google Account**.

2. **Navigate to Security Settings:**

   - Tap the **Security** tab and scroll down to find the **Signing in to Google** section.

3. **Enable Two-Step Verification:**

   - Tap **2-Step Verification** and follow the on-screen instructions to set it up.

- o You'll be asked to enter your Google account password, and then you'll choose a second step—either a **phone number** for text messages or an **Authenticator app** for generating codes.

4. **Complete Setup:**

- o After setting up 2FA, Google will require you to enter a code sent to your phone or generated by your app whenever you sign in.

Managing App Permissions

Control which apps have access to your personal data with the App Permissions feature in Android 14.

Managing App Permissions:

1. **Open Settings:**

- o Go to **Settings > Privacy > Permission manager**.

2. **Select Permission Type:**

- o You will see categories like **Location, Camera, Microphone**, etc. Tap on a category to view which apps have permission to use that feature.

3. **Manage Permissions:**

- o Select an app and choose whether to allow or deny its permission to access that feature. For example, if you don't want an app to access your **Location**, tap on it and select **Deny**.

4. **Review Permissions Regularly:**

   o It's a good idea to periodically review these settings to ensure your privacy is maintained.

How to Use VPN for Privacy

A VPN (Virtual Private Network) encrypts your internet connection, providing privacy when browsing online.

Setting Up a VPN:

1. **Open Settings:**

   o Go to **Settings** > **Network & Internet** > **VPN**.

2. **Add VPN:**

   o Tap **Add VPN** and enter the required information from your VPN provider (such as server address, your username, and password).

3. **Connect to VPN:**

   o Once the VPN is configured, tap the **VPN name** to connect to it. You'll see a key icon in the status bar when connected.

4. **Disconnecting from VPN:**

   o To disconnect, tap on the **VPN** option again and select **Disconnect**.

Privacy Settings: Enabling Encryption and Secure Folders

Android 14 offers encryption options that protect your data in case your device is lost or stolen. You can also use **Secure Folders** to store sensitive files.

Enabling Encryption:

1. **Go to Settings:**

   o   Go to **Settings > Security > Encryption & Credentials**.

2. **Encrypt Your Device:**

   o   If encryption isn't already enabled, you will see the option to **Encrypt your device**. Tap it to begin encryption, which ensures your data is secure if someone tries to access it.

Using Secure Folders:

1. **Create a Secure Folder:**

   o   Go to **Settings > Security > Secure Folder**.

   o   Tap **Create Secure Folder** and set a password for it.

2. **Add Files to the Secure Folder:**

   o   Move photos, videos, and documents into the folder for extra privacy. These files will be encrypted and accessible only through your Secure Folder password.

Managing Security Updates and Patches

Keeping your phone's software up to date is crucial for maintaining security.

Checking for Updates:

1. **Open Settings:**

   o Go to **Settings** > **System** > **Updates**.

2. **Check for Updates:**

   o Tap on **Check for updates**. If a new update is available, follow the on-screen prompts to download and install it.

3. **Enable Auto Updates:**

   o For automatic updates, ensure that **Automatic updates** is enabled. This will allow your phone to download and install security patches without your intervention.

Locking Apps with Biometrics

Locking individual apps for extra privacy can prevent unauthorized access to your apps.

Locking Apps:

1. **Open Settings:**

   o Go to **Settings** > **Security** > **App Lock**.

2. **Enable App Lock:**

   o Turn on **App Lock** and choose the apps you want to lock.

3. **Use Fingerprint or Face Unlock:**

   o Select **Fingerprint** or **Face Unlock** as the method to access these apps. Now, whenever you open a locked app, you'll need to use biometrics to gain access.

How to Track Your Phone if Lost

If your **Motorola Razr Plus 2025** is lost or stolen, you can track it through Google's **Find My Device**.

Enabling Find My Device:

1. **Open Settings:**

   o Go to **Settings** > **Security** > **Find My Device**.

2. **Enable Find My Device:**

   o Make sure **Find My Device** is turned on. This will allow you to locate your phone through your Google account.

3. **Tracking Your Phone:**

   o Visit **https://www.google.com/android/find** from any browser, sign in with your Google account, and you can see your phone's location on a map.

4. **Lock or Erase Your Device:**

o   From the **Find My Device** page, you can also remotely lock your phone or erase all data if you're concerned about your privacy.

By following these steps, your **Motorola Razr Plus 2025** will be as secure as possible. Regularly review your security settings and stay up-to-date with software updates to ensure your phone is protected.

Gaming on the Motorola Razr Plus

Gaming on your **Motorola Razr Plus 2025** is a fantastic experience, thanks to its powerful hardware, high-quality display, and customizable performance settings. This chapter will walk you through everything you need to know to enhance your gaming experience on your Razr Plus, from optimizing settings to using external controllers and game streaming features.

By the end of this chapter, you'll be ready to dive into your favorite games with the best performance possible.

Optimizing Your Phone for Gaming Performance

Before jumping into any game, it's a good idea to optimize your **Motorola Razr Plus** for the best gaming experience. This involves adjusting a few settings that will help boost performance and reduce distractions.

Step-by-Step:

1. **Close Unnecessary Apps:**

   o   Tap the **Recent Apps** button (usually the square icon on the bottom of the screen).

   o   Swipe away any apps you aren't currently using to free up resources and memory for gaming.

2. **Enable Battery Saver Mode:**

   o   Open the **Settings** app.

o   Scroll down and tap on **Battery**.

o   Toggle **Battery Saver** on if your phone's battery is running low to reduce power consumption and ensure smoother gaming.

3. **Adjust Display Settings:**

o   Go to **Settings** > **Display**.

o   Increase the **Brightness** to make sure you can see your games clearly.

o   Optionally, turn off **Adaptive Brightness** to keep the brightness at a consistent level during gaming.

4. **Ensure Your Phone is Connected to Wi-Fi:**

o   For online gaming, make sure you're connected to a strong and stable Wi-Fi network to avoid lag. You can check Wi-Fi settings by swiping down on your home screen and ensuring the Wi-Fi symbol is active.

5. **Activate Performance Mode (if available):**

o   Go to **Settings** > **Battery** > **Performance Mode** (if this option is available).

o   Toggle it on for maximum performance when gaming. This ensures your phone uses all of its available power to give you a smoother gaming experience.

Installing and Using Game Apps

To get started, you'll first need to download and install your favorite game apps. The **Google Play Store** has a wide variety of games, from casual to highly immersive experiences.

Step-by-Step:

1. **Open the Google Play Store:**

   o Tap on the **Play Store** app on your home screen or app drawer.

2. **Search for Games:**

   o Tap the **Search bar** at the top and type in the name of the game you want to play (for example, "PUBG Mobile," "Call of Duty Mobile," or "Candy Crush").

   o Press **Enter** or tap on the **Search icon** to view the results.

3. **Install the Game:**

   o Tap on the game you want to install from the search results.

   o Tap the **Install** button to begin downloading the game.

   o Once installed, you'll see the **Open** button. Tap it to launch the game.

4. **Sign Into Your Game Account (if necessary):**

- Many games require you to log in using a social media account (like Facebook or Google) or create a new account.

- Follow the on-screen instructions to set up your profile and start playing.

Enabling Gaming Mode for Better Performance

Gaming Mode is a feature that prioritizes resources for gaming, making sure no notifications or background processes interfere with your experience.

Step-by-Step:

1. **Open the Settings app:**

   - Tap the **Settings** icon from your home screen or app drawer.

2. **Go to 'Gaming' or 'Moto Actions':**

   - Scroll down and select **Gaming**. If you don't see it, tap on **Moto Actions** and look for the **Gaming Mode** option.

3. **Enable Gaming Mode:**

   - Once in the Gaming section, find **Gaming Mode** and toggle it on.

   - You can also customize the behavior by turning on **Do Not Disturb** (which silences notifications) and **Performance Boost** to ensure the best gameplay experience.

4. **Access Quick Settings During Gaming:**

   o While gaming, you can swipe down from the top of the screen to access **Gaming Mode settings** quickly. This lets you turn features on/off without interrupting your gameplay.

Enhancing Game Graphics and Responsiveness

To get the best visual experience and ensure your games run smoothly, you may want to tweak a few additional settings.

Step-by-Step:

1. **Adjust Game Graphics Settings (Inside the Game):**

   o Many games have an in-game graphics settings menu. Look for an option such as **Graphics, Video Settings**, or **Display**.

   o Choose the highest graphical quality your phone can handle. If you experience lag or slowdowns, try lowering the graphics quality to **Medium** or **Low** to boost performance.

2. **Enable 'High Refresh Rate' (if available):**

   o The **Motorola Razr Plus 2025** comes with a smooth display that supports high refresh rates. Go to **Settings** > **Display** > **Refresh Rate** and set it to the highest option available (usually **90Hz** or

120Hz). This will make your games feel smoother and more responsive.

3. **Use Game Mode to Maximize Performance:**

   o As mentioned earlier, enabling **Gaming Mode** ensures that your phone focuses resources on your game. This should automatically adjust settings for optimal gaming performance.

Using External Game Controllers with Razr Plus

For a more immersive gaming experience, you can connect a **Bluetooth game controller** to your **Motorola Razr Plus 2025**. This is perfect for games that support controller input, giving you more precision and control.

Step-by-Step:

1. **Turn on Your Game Controller:**

   o Follow the instructions for your specific controller to turn it on and enter **Pairing Mode**. Typically, this involves holding down a button until the controller's LED light flashes.

2. **Open Bluetooth Settings on Your Phone:**

   o Go to **Settings** > **Connected Devices** > **Bluetooth**.

   o Toggle **Bluetooth** on if it's not already enabled.

3. **Pair Your Controller:**

o   Your controller should appear in the list of available devices. Tap on it to pair your controller with your phone.

o   Once paired, your controller should vibrate or show a steady light to confirm the connection.

4. **Launch Your Game:**

o   Open the game you want to play, and the controller should automatically be recognized. If the game supports controllers, you can start playing right away.

Tip: Popular controllers such as the **Xbox Wireless Controller** and **PlayStation DualShock** controllers work great with the **Motorola Razr Plus**.

Game Streaming Features: Play on TV or PC

With the **Motorola Razr Plus**, you can play games on larger screens like your **TV** or **PC**. Game streaming lets you experience your mobile games on a bigger, more immersive display.

Step-by-Step:

1. **Use Google Cast (for TV):**

o   Ensure your **TV** supports Google Cast (or a Chromecast device is connected).

o   Swipe down from the top of your phone's screen and tap the **Cast** icon.

- Select your **TV** from the list of available devices to mirror your phone's display.

- Start your game, and it will be streamed to your TV.

2. **Use Steam Link (for PC):**

- Install the **Steam Link** app from the **Google Play Store** on your **Motorola Razr Plus**.

- Connect your phone and PC to the same Wi-Fi network.

- Open Steam Link on your phone and follow the setup instructions to connect to your **PC**.

- Once connected, you can play your PC games using your phone.

Popular Game Recommendations for the Razr Plus

Here are some popular games that will perform excellently on the **Motorola Razr Plus**:

1. **PUBG Mobile:** A fast-paced battle royale game that benefits from the phone's smooth display and gaming mode.

2. **Call of Duty Mobile:** High-action shooter with great controller support and a variety of game modes.

3. **Genshin Impact:** An open-world adventure game that looks amazing on your Razr Plus's high-resolution display.

4. **Asphalt 9: Legends:** A fast-paced racing game that will take full advantage of the phone's graphics and performance.

Tip: Always check the minimum device requirements for games in the **Google Play Store** to ensure optimal performance.

With these steps, you're now equipped to get the most out of your **Motorola Razr Plus 2025** for gaming. Whether you're enjoying games on your phone, connecting a controller, or even streaming to a larger screen, you can enjoy top-tier gaming experiences right from your device.

By optimizing your phone's settings, adjusting in-game graphics, and using accessories like controllers, your **Razr Plus** is ready for action-packed gameplay anytime. Happy gaming!

Battery Management and Optimization

Battery life is one of the most important aspects of your **Motorola Razr Plus 2025**, especially when you're on the go. Proper battery management can help you get the most out of your device throughout the day, ensuring that you can use it for calls, texts, gaming, and more without worrying about running out of power.

This chapter will guide you through all the necessary steps for managing battery life, optimizing energy consumption, and getting the best performance out of your phone's battery. Whether you're a beginner or an experienced user, this guide will provide all the information you need to keep your phone powered up.

Charging Your Motorola Razr Plus

Understanding the proper way to charge your **Motorola Razr Plus** is essential to ensure its long-term health and optimal battery performance.

Step-by-Step:

1. **Using the Charger Provided in the Box:**

   o Your **Motorola Razr Plus** comes with a **USB-C charging cable** and a **charging adapter** in the box. To ensure the best charging speed, always use the charger that came with the phone or a reputable third-party charger with a **fast-charging** feature.

2. **Plugging In Your Charger:**

   o Insert the **USB-C end** of the charging cable into the charging port at the bottom of your phone.

   o Plug the other end into the **charging adapter** and then into a **power outlet**.

3. **Wireless Charging (if supported):**

   o The **Motorola Razr Plus** supports **Qi wireless charging**, allowing you to charge your phone without needing to plug it in.

   o Place your phone on a compatible **Qi wireless charger**. Ensure the charger is plugged into a power source.

   o Make sure your phone is aligned with the wireless charger, and you should see the charging indicator appear on your screen.

4. **Charging Tips:**

   o Avoid letting your phone get to **0%** too often. Try to keep it charged between **20% and 80%** for optimal battery health.

   o When charging, it's best to keep your phone on a flat surface and avoid using it heavily, as using the phone while charging can generate more heat and may affect the charging process.

How to Use Battery Saver Mode

Battery Saver Mode is a feature that helps extend your phone's battery life by limiting background processes, notifications, and other power-consuming activities.

Step-by-Step:

1. **Access Battery Saver Mode:**

   o Open the **Settings** app on your **Motorola Razr Plus**.

   o Scroll down and tap on **Battery**.

   o Tap on **Battery Saver**.

2. **Turning on Battery Saver Mode:**

   o Toggle the **Battery Saver** switch to turn it on.

   o This will limit background activity, reduce the screen brightness, and disable non-essential apps and services to save power.

3. **Customizing Battery Saver Mode:**

   o You can set **Battery Saver Mode** to turn on automatically when your battery reaches a specific percentage (e.g., 15%).

   o Tap on **Turn On Automatically** and set your preferred threshold.

4. **Activating Battery Saver Mode from Quick Settings:**

   o   Swipe down from the top of your screen to access **Quick Settings**.

   o   Tap on the **Battery Saver icon** (a battery icon with a downward arrow) to activate the mode quickly.

Optimizing Battery Life

To ensure your phone's battery lasts throughout the day, you can optimize various settings and features that affect power consumption.

Step-by-Step:

1. **Adjust Screen Brightness:**

   o   Open **Settings** > **Display**.

   o   Lower the **Brightness** manually or enable **Adaptive Brightness**, which adjusts the screen brightness based on your surroundings.

2. **Disable Unused Features:**

   o   **Bluetooth**: If you're not using Bluetooth, turn it off by swiping down the **Quick Settings** menu and tapping the **Bluetooth icon**.

   o   **Location Services**: Turn off **Location** services when not needed by going to **Settings** > **Location** and toggling it off.

3. **Use Dark Mode:**

- o **Dark Mode** reduces the energy your phone uses, especially on OLED screens like the one on your Razr Plus.

- o Go to **Settings** > **Display** > **Theme** and toggle **Dark Mode** on.

4. **Turn Off Always-On Display:**

- o If you're not using the **Always-On Display** feature, go to **Settings** > **Display** > **Always On Display** and turn it off to save battery.

Apps That Drain Your Battery: Managing Power-hungry Apps

Certain apps consume a lot of battery life. Identifying and managing these apps can help you extend the time between charges.

Step-by-Step:

1. **View Battery Usage:**

- o Go to **Settings** > **Battery** > **Battery Usage** to see which apps are consuming the most power.

2. **Managing Power-hungry Apps:**

- o For apps that use excessive battery, consider the following:

  - ▪ **Close apps** when you're not using them.

- **Uninstall** apps that you rarely use.

- **Update** apps regularly to benefit from optimizations that might reduce power consumption.

3. **Disable Background Activity for Certain Apps:**

    o Go to **Settings** > **Apps** > **[App Name]** > **Battery** and select **Restricted** to limit the app's background activities, reducing battery usage.

Using Energy-Efficient Settings

Energy-efficient settings can help you conserve battery without sacrificing performance.

Step-by-Step:

1. **Enable Adaptive Battery:**

    o Go to **Settings** > **Battery** > **Adaptive Battery** and toggle it on.

    o Adaptive Battery learns your usage habits and limits power to apps you don't use often.

2. **Reduce Screen Timeout:**

    o Go to **Settings** > **Display** > **Screen Timeout**.

    o Set a shorter time (e.g., **15 or 30 seconds**) for your phone to automatically turn off the screen when not in use.

3. **Disable Vibrations:**

   o Vibrations use extra power. To turn them off, go to **Settings** > **Sound** and toggle off **Vibrate on touch** and **Vibrate for calls**.

Understanding Battery Health and Lifespan

To maintain battery health, it's important to understand how to take care of your battery and what affects its lifespan over time.

Step-by-Step:

1. **What Affects Battery Health?**

   o **Heat**: Avoid charging or using your phone in extremely hot environments. Excess heat can degrade the battery over time.

   o **Frequent Full Charges**: It's ideal to keep your battery between **20-80%** for longevity.

2. **Battery Health Status:**

   o While **Motorola Razr Plus** doesn't have a direct "battery health" feature, you can still monitor the battery's behavior. If your phone consistently drains faster than normal or doesn't charge properly, it may indicate a need for battery replacement.

Wireless Charging and Battery Tips

Using **wireless charging** is convenient, but it does require some extra attention to ensure the best performance.

Step-by-Step:

1. **Using Wireless Charging:**

    o   Place your phone correctly on a **Qi-compatible wireless charger**.

    o   Ensure that the charging pad is plugged in and aligned with your phone's charging coil.

2. **Charging Tips:**

    o   Wireless charging is slower than wired charging. Use it when you don't need a quick charge, like overnight.

    o   Don't use your phone while it's wirelessly charging, as it can generate heat and reduce efficiency.

Power Saving Tips for Long Trips

If you're going on a long trip, follow these tips to maximize your **Motorola Razr Plus**'s battery life.

Step-by-Step:

1. **Enable Battery Saver Mode:**

o   Make sure **Battery Saver Mode** is on, as it will extend battery life by limiting unnecessary processes.

2. **Download Offline Content:**

    o   Download music, movies, and maps for offline use, so you don't need to stream or use data during your trip.

3. **Turn Off Unnecessary Features:**

    o   Turn off **Wi-Fi**, **Bluetooth**, and **Location Services** when you're not using them. You can do this quickly by swiping down the **Quick Settings** menu.

4. **Use Airplane Mode (When Necessary):**

    o   If you don't need to be connected to cellular networks or Wi-Fi, enable **Airplane Mode** to conserve battery during long periods of non-use.

With these tips, you can ensure that your **Motorola Razr Plus 2025** has the best possible battery life and performance, whether you're playing games, watching videos, or just using your phone for everyday tasks. By managing your battery settings, charging properly, and optimizing your phone's features, you'll be able to enjoy your device to the fullest without constantly worrying about running out of power.

Troubleshooting and FAQ

Even the best smartphones can encounter issues from time to time. The Motorola Razr Plus is a powerful and reliable device, but you may run into minor problems like screen flickering, app crashes, or connectivity issues. In this chapter, we will guide you step by step through troubleshooting common problems, as well as offer solutions to improve your phone's performance.

Common Problems and Solutions

Let's first go over some of the most common problems users may encounter with their Motorola Razr Plus, and the solutions to fix them.

- **App Crashes**: If apps are crashing or not responding, it could be due to outdated software, app bugs, or insufficient storage space.

    o **Solution**: Try closing and reopening the app. If it continues to crash, check for app updates in the Google Play Store. Also, ensure your phone's software is up-to-date by going to **Settings > Software Update**.

- **Screen Flickering**: A flickering screen can occur due to software glitches, too many apps running in the background, or low display settings.

    o **Solution**: Restart your phone. If the issue persists, go to **Settings > Display** and reduce the brightness or change the screen refresh rate if your phone supports it.

- **Battery Draining Quickly**: Sometimes, users notice that the battery drains quickly even when the phone isn't being used heavily.

  - **Solution**: Go to **Settings > Battery** to see which apps are consuming the most power. Try disabling background data for power-hungry apps, turn on **Battery Saver**, and enable **Adaptive Battery**.

How to Fix Screen Flickering or Touch Issues

A flickering screen or unresponsive touch issues can be frustrating, but here's how to resolve them:

1. **Restart Your Phone**: Sometimes, simply restarting the device can resolve minor software glitches.

2. **Adjust Screen Brightness**: Excessive brightness may cause flickering, especially in low-light conditions.

   - Go to **Settings > Display**.

   - Enable **Adaptive Brightness** or adjust the brightness manually.

3. **Check for Updates**: Software updates often contain bug fixes for display issues. Go to **Settings > Software Update** and make sure your phone is up-to-date.

4. **Reset Display Settings**: If you've made custom adjustments to the display settings, it might be worth resetting them to default. You can find the

reset option under **Settings** > **Display** > **Advanced**.

5. **Clear the Cache**: Sometimes, clearing the cache can resolve issues with unresponsive screens.

   o Go to **Settings > Apps > [App Name] > Storage** and select **Clear Cache**.

Resolving Performance Lag or Freezing

If your Motorola Razr Plus is lagging or freezing during use, here's a simple step-by-step guide to resolve it:

1. **Close Unnecessary Apps**:

   o Press the **Recent Apps** button (usually the square button at the bottom).

   o Swipe away any apps you're not actively using to free up memory.

2. **Clear App Cache**:

   o Some apps store data in their cache, which can slow down performance. To clear it, go to **Settings > Apps > [App Name] > Storage** and tap **Clear Cache**.

3. **Reboot Your Phone**: If your phone is freezing or lagging, try restarting it to clear temporary files and refresh the system.

4. **Free Up Storage**: Lack of available storage can cause your phone to slow down.

- Go to **Settings > Storage** and see how much space is available.

- Remove unnecessary files or move them to cloud storage or an SD card if supported.

5. **Factory Reset**: If lag continues despite your efforts, consider a **Factory Reset**. This will erase all data from your phone, so make sure to back up your data before proceeding.

- Go to **Settings > System > Reset > Factory Data Reset**.

What to Do if the Phone Overheats

Overheating is a sign that your phone might be running too many apps or processes at once, or it could be due to environmental factors.

1. **Close Background Apps**: Apps running in the background use processing power and can cause the phone to heat up. Close unnecessary apps by going to **Recent Apps** and swiping them away.

2. **Remove the Case**: If your phone is in a case, it can trap heat. Remove the case to help cool the phone down.

3. **Turn Off Power-Intensive Features**: Disable features like **GPS, Bluetooth**, or **Wi-Fi** when you're not using them.

4. **Avoid Direct Sunlight**: Make sure your phone is not in direct sunlight for long periods, as this can cause it to overheat.

5. **Reboot the Device**: Sometimes a restart can help reset any overheating processes and bring the temperature back to normal.

Resolving Connectivity Issues (Wi-Fi, Bluetooth, Cellular)

If you're facing issues with Wi-Fi, Bluetooth, or cellular connectivity, follow these steps to troubleshoot:

Wi-Fi Issues

1. **Restart Your Router**: Sometimes the issue lies with the router. Unplug it, wait for 30 seconds, and plug it back in.

2. **Forget and Reconnect to Wi-Fi**:

   o   Go to **Settings > Wi-Fi**.

   o   Tap on the Wi-Fi network you're having trouble with and select **Forget**.

   o   Then reconnect by selecting the network again and entering the password.

3. **Check Airplane Mode**: Ensure that **Airplane Mode** is turned off in **Settings > Network & Internet**.

Bluetooth Issues

1. **Restart Bluetooth**: Toggle Bluetooth off and back on in **Settings > Bluetooth**.

2. **Forget and Reconnect Devices**: If a Bluetooth device isn't connecting properly, go to **Settings > Bluetooth**, select the device, and tap **Forget**. Then pair it again.

Cellular Connectivity Issues

1. **Toggle Airplane Mode**: Switching **Airplane Mode** on and off can reset network connections. Go to **Settings > Network & Internet** to toggle it.

2. **Check Network Coverage**: Make sure you're in an area with good cellular coverage. If not, try moving to a different location.

3. **Contact Carrier**: If the issue persists, it might be a network problem. Reach out to your carrier for assistance.

Troubleshooting Camera Issues

If your camera isn't working correctly, try the following:

1. **Restart the Camera App**: Close the camera app and reopen it to see if that resolves the issue.

2. **Check for Obstructions**: Make sure the camera lenses are clean and not obstructed by dirt or debris.

3. **Check for Software Updates**: Ensure the camera app is updated in the Google Play Store and that your phone's software is up to date.

4. **Clear Camera App Cache**:

o Go to **Settings > Apps > Camera > Storage** and tap **Clear Cache**.

5. **Reset Camera Settings**: If there's an issue with specific camera settings, reset them to default by going to **Settings > Camera > Reset Settings**.

Restoring Your Phone to Factory Settings

If all else fails and you want to start fresh, restoring your Motorola Razr Plus to its original factory settings may help.

1. **Backup Your Data**: Make sure to back up your photos, videos, contacts, and other important data before performing a factory reset.

   o You can back up your data using Google Drive, Google Photos, or Motorola's backup options.

2. **Perform the Reset**:

   o Go to **Settings > System > Reset > Factory Data Reset**.

   o Tap **Erase All Data** and confirm. Your phone will restart and return to its factory settings.

Note: A factory reset will erase all your data, so be sure you have backed up everything important beforehand.

When to Contact Motorola Support

If the troubleshooting steps above don't resolve your issue, or if your phone is still under warranty, it's a good idea to reach out to Motorola Support.

1. **Visit Motorola's Support Website**: You can find solutions to many problems on their official support website.

2. **Use the Motorola Support App**: The Motorola Support app provides easy access to solutions and allows you to contact support directly.

3. **Contact via Phone or Chat**: If needed, you can call or chat with a support representative for further assistance.

FAQ (Frequently Asked Questions)

Q1: How do I turn on the flashlight on the Motorola Razr Plus?

- Swipe down from the top of the screen to open the Quick Settings menu. Tap the **Flashlight** icon.

Q2: How do I take a screenshot?

- Press and hold the **Power button** and **Volume Down button** simultaneously for a couple of seconds to take a screenshot.

Q3: Why is my phone not charging?

- Check if the charging cable is properly connected and if the charger works with another device. Also, make sure the charging port is clean.

Q4: How do I use Google Assistant?

- Hold the **Home button** or say "Hey Google" to activate Google Assistant.

This section covers the most common issues you might face with your Motorola Razr Plus and provides clear solutions to fix them. Troubleshooting doesn't have to be frustrating – with these steps, you can easily resolve most problems. If you encounter any other issues or need more help, feel free to ask. I'm here to assist you and make sure your phone runs smoothly!

Advanced Features & Tips

This chapter is designed for users who want to take their Motorola Razr Plus to the next level. Whether you're interested in customizing the device, improving performance, or exploring advanced settings, we'll walk you through the process step by step, in a simple and beginner-friendly way. By the end of this chapter, you'll be able to explore features and settings that let you personalize your Razr Plus like a pro.

Using Developer Mode for Advanced Customization

Developer Mode is a special setting on Android devices that unlocks a wide range of features for customization and debugging. Don't worry; you don't need to be an expert to enable Developer Mode—it's just a matter of following a few simple steps.

How to enable Developer Mode on your Motorola Razr Plus:

1. **Open the Settings app**: From the home screen, swipe up and tap on the gear icon to access your settings.

2. **Scroll down and tap "About phone"**: This section contains all the important information about your device.

3. **Find the "Build number"**: Scroll down until you see "Build number."

4. **Tap the Build number seven times**: You'll see a message saying, "You are now a developer."

It's that simple! Now you can access Developer Options from your settings.

What you can do in Developer Mode:

- **Enable USB Debugging**: This is essential for connecting your phone to a computer for more advanced features.

- **Modify animation speeds**: You can speed up or slow down animations to make your device feel snappier or more fluid.

- **Stay awake**: Your screen won't automatically turn off while charging, making it handy for long tasks.

Tip: Be cautious when making changes in Developer Mode. Some settings can affect your phone's performance or battery life.

Rooting Your Device (For Advanced Users)

Rooting your Motorola Razr Plus gives you access to the Android system files and enables you to customize and tweak your phone like never before. However, this is **not recommended for beginners**, as it can void your warranty and possibly cause issues if done incorrectly. If you decide to root, do so with caution.

Why root your device?

- **Full control over the system**: You can remove pre-installed apps (bloatware) and make deeper customizations.

- **Access to root-only apps**: Some apps require root access to function, offering you additional features.

Steps for rooting (for advanced users only):

1. **Backup Your Data**: Rooting will wipe your phone. Make sure to back up everything important, like photos, contacts, and messages.

2. **Unlock the Bootloader**: This is the first step in rooting. Motorola has a tool for unlocking the bootloader (find it on their official website).

3. **Install Custom Recovery**: You'll need a custom recovery like TWRP (Team Win Recovery Project) to install a root package.

4. **Flash the Root Package**: After installing the recovery, you'll flash the root package onto your device, which gives you full system access.

Important Note: Rooting can cause your phone to become less stable or even brick it if done incorrectly. Always follow trusted guides from experienced users.

Custom ROMs and Enhancing Your Android Experience

Custom ROMs are alternative versions of the Android operating system, often offering more features, better performance, or a completely different user interface. Installing a custom ROM lets you tailor your phone to your preferences.

How to install a custom ROM:

1. **Backup your data**: Just like rooting, installing a custom ROM will wipe everything. Backup your photos, apps, and settings first.

2. **Unlock your bootloader**: This step is the same as rooting your device (refer to section 12.2).

3. **Download the ROM**: Find a custom ROM that's compatible with your Motorola Razr Plus. Popular ones include LineageOS and Pixel Experience.

4. **Install a custom recovery**: You'll need to install TWRP or another recovery tool.

5. **Flash the ROM**: In recovery mode, select the "Install" option and choose the ROM you downloaded. Confirm the installation, and the ROM will be installed.

Tip: Research your ROM before installing it. Some ROMs may have bugs or compatibility issues, so make sure it's well-tested on your device.

Using Android Debug Bridge (ADB)

ADB (Android Debug Bridge) is a powerful tool that allows you to communicate with your Motorola Razr Plus through your computer. It's used to run commands, install apps, and perform a variety of other tasks.

How to use ADB:

1. **Enable Developer Mode and USB Debugging**: Follow the steps in Section 12.1 to enable Developer Mode and USB Debugging.

2. **Install ADB on your PC**: You'll need to download and install ADB on your computer. You can find the official installation guide on Google's website.

3. **Connect your phone to the computer**: Use a USB cable to connect your Razr Plus to your computer.

4. **Open Command Prompt or Terminal**: On your computer, open a command prompt (Windows) or terminal (Mac/Linux).

5. **Use ADB commands**: You can use various ADB commands to interact with your device, such as installing apps or pulling system logs.

Example Command:

If you want to install an APK from your computer to your phone, you'd type:

```
adb install [path_to_apk]
```

Managing Hidden Settings in Android 14

Android 14 has plenty of settings hidden within menus that most users never notice. These settings can allow you to customize your device further and improve performance.

How to access hidden settings:

1. **Enable Developer Mode**: As explained earlier, you'll need to enable Developer Mode first.

2. **Use the Secret Settings Code**: For example, typing *#*#4636#*#* into the dialer can bring up information about your phone's battery, network, and usage stats.

3. **Hidden System Settings**: There are hidden options within Android 14 to control things like network speed, background processes, and system animations.

Tip: Use these settings sparingly. While they can enhance your device's performance, messing with certain options can lead to instability.

Optimizing System Performance with Advanced Settings

There are numerous ways to optimize your Motorola Razr Plus for better performance, especially if you want to speed things up or conserve battery life.

Steps for optimization:

1. **Use Developer Mode**: In Developer Mode, you can tweak settings like animation speed and limit background processes, which can make your device feel faster.

2. **Disable or Uninstall Bloatware**: Some pre-installed apps aren't necessary. You can disable or uninstall them from the "Apps & notifications" section of settings.

3. **Limit Background Apps**: Go to Settings > Battery > Battery Saver, and enable it to reduce the background activity of apps.

Tip: Don't over-optimize. Sometimes, too many tweaks can cause the phone to behave erratically.

Exploring the advanced features of your Motorola Razr Plus opens up a world of possibilities. From tweaking the system settings to unlocking your phone's full potential with custom ROMs, there's a lot you can do. Just be sure to follow each step carefully and always back up your data before making any major changes.

If you want to take full advantage of the Razr Plus's capabilities, experimenting with these advanced settings and features will certainly enhance your experience. However, remember that many of these changes are for power users, so proceed with caution and enjoy your customization journey!

Health, Wellness, and Emergency Features

Your Motorola Razr Plus isn't just a tool for communication—it's also packed with features that can help you manage your health, wellness, and safety. Whether you're looking to track your fitness, prepare for an emergency, or practice mindful digital well-being, this chapter will guide you through the essential features that keep you safe and healthy.

Fitness and Health Apps on Your Motorola Razr Plus

Your phone has a lot of fitness and wellness features built into it, but the key apps are a great way to keep track of your health and physical activities. Here's how to get started with them:

How to access and use fitness and health apps:

1. **Google Fit**

   Google Fit is a popular fitness tracking app available on Android devices, including your Razr Plus. It tracks your activity, heart rate, steps, and even your sleep.

   o **Install Google Fit** (if not already installed):

     ▪ Open the **Google Play Store**.

     ▪ Search for **Google Fit**.

- Tap **Install** and wait for the app to download and install.

- o **Set up Google Fit**:

  - Once installed, open the app, and sign in with your Google account.

  - Allow the app to access your device's sensors (steps, heart rate, etc.).

  - Set your fitness goals, like steps per day or exercise minutes, based on your fitness level.

  - Use the app regularly to track activities like walking, running, cycling, and more.

2. **Third-party Fitness Apps**

If you prefer more specialized tracking, there are numerous third-party apps like **Strava**, **MyFitnessPal**, or **Samsung Health** that you can download from the Play Store.

- o **Download a third-party app**:

  - Open **Google Play Store**.

  - Search for your desired fitness app (e.g., **Strava**).

  - Tap **Install** and follow the on-screen instructions to sign up and start tracking your activities.

Tip: Make sure to enable the appropriate permissions for these apps so they can track your steps, heart rate, and activities accurately.

Setting Up Emergency Information for First Responders

In case of an emergency, it's important that first responders have access to key information like your medical history, allergies, and emergency contacts. Your Motorola Razr Plus lets you easily set up this information.

How to set up Emergency Information:

1. **Open the Settings app**:

   o Swipe up from the home screen and tap on the **gear icon** to open Settings.

2. **Go to the "Emergency" section**:

   o Scroll down and tap on **Emergency** or **Emergency Information** (this may vary based on your device).

3. **Fill in your emergency details**:

   o Tap **Add information** to enter important medical details such as:

      ▪ Allergies

      ▪ Blood type

      ▪ Medical conditions

      ▪ Medications you are currently taking

- Emergency contacts (these will be listed in case someone needs to contact your family or friends)

4. **Activate the emergency lock screen feature**:

   o You can choose to display this information directly on the lock screen for easy access in case of an emergency. To do this:

     - Turn on **"Show emergency information on lock screen"**.

Once set up, first responders can access this information directly from your locked screen by swiping up, without needing to unlock your phone.

Using the Emergency SOS Feature

The Emergency SOS feature on your Motorola Razr Plus is a lifesaver in situations where you need to quickly alert others or seek help. Here's how it works:

How to set up and use the Emergency SOS feature:

1. **Enable Emergency SOS:**

   o Open the **Settings app**.

   o Scroll down and tap on **Safety & Emergency**.

   o Tap **Emergency SOS** to turn it on.

   o Customize settings like:

     - **Send SOS messages**: You can select emergency contacts to send an alert when you activate the SOS feature.

- **Call emergency services**: You can also configure your phone to automatically dial emergency services when you activate SOS.

2. **Activating Emergency SOS**:

   o To activate the SOS feature, press the **power button** five times quickly in succession.

   o Your phone will automatically send your location and an SOS message to your pre-selected contacts, and in some cases, it will call emergency services.

Tip: Practice activating Emergency SOS to ensure you're comfortable using it quickly when needed.

How to Monitor Your Fitness with Google Fit

Google Fit is a great tool for anyone looking to stay active. It uses your phone's built-in sensors to track your activity, helping you stay on top of your fitness goals.

How to use Google Fit effectively:

1. **Track steps and activity**:

   o Google Fit automatically tracks your steps as you walk. It uses your phone's accelerometer to monitor your movements and record them as part of your daily activity log.

2. **Set fitness goals**:

    o   Open the **Google Fit** app, tap the **Profile icon** in the top right corner, and select **Fitness Goals**.

    o   You can set goals like walking **10,000 steps per day** or engaging in **30 minutes of exercise** daily.

3. **Track workouts**:

    o   Google Fit can track a variety of activities such as running, cycling, and hiking. To start tracking an activity:

        ▪   Open **Google Fit**, tap **Start workout**, and select the type of activity.

        ▪   Google Fit will track the duration, distance, and calories burned.

4. **Monitor heart rate and sleep**:

    o   If your Motorola Razr Plus is paired with a compatible fitness tracker or smartwatch, Google Fit can also monitor your **heart rate** and **sleep patterns**.

Tip: Regularly check the **Journal** tab in Google Fit to see your progress and analyze trends over time.

Tips for Managing Your Digital Wellbeing

Digital well-being tools help you balance your screen time, practice mindfulness, and focus on what's important in your daily life.

How to manage Digital Wellbeing on your Motorola Razr Plus:

1. **Set Screen Time Limits**:

   o Open the **Settings app**, scroll down to **Digital Wellbeing & Parental Controls**.

   o Tap on **Dashboard** to view which apps you use the most.

   o From there, you can set daily time limits for each app to help manage your screen time.

2. **Use Focus Mode**:

   o If you find it hard to concentrate due to constant notifications, try Focus Mode.

   o Open **Digital Wellbeing > Focus Mode > Turn on Focus Mode**.

   o Select the apps you want to pause, and focus on the task at hand without distractions.

3. **Wind Down Mode**:

o If you have trouble sleeping because of late-night phone use, Wind Down Mode is helpful.

o Go to **Digital Wellbeing** > **Bedtime mode**, and set a time for when your phone should reduce blue light and mute notifications.

4. **Use Do Not Disturb**:

o To avoid distractions during important times, enable **Do Not Disturb**.

o Go to **Settings** > **Sound** > **Do Not Disturb**, and choose when to silence calls, texts, and app notifications.

Your Motorola Razr Plus offers a lot of features to help you stay healthy, manage your wellness, and keep you safe in emergencies. Whether you're tracking your fitness with Google Fit, setting up emergency contacts, or using the SOS feature to alert others, the phone can be a crucial tool for your overall well-being.

Always take a moment to explore these features, set them up properly, and use them when needed. A well-prepared phone not only keeps you connected but also ensures your health and safety. If you have any questions or need assistance with setting up any of these features, don't hesitate to ask!

Motorola Accessories and Ecosystem Integration

Motorola offers a variety of accessories that can enhance your experience with the Motorola Razr Plus. Whether you're looking for better sound, enhanced fitness tracking, or a seamless connection to other devices, Motorola's ecosystem can help you do it all. In this chapter, we'll walk you through the best accessories and explain how to integrate them with your Razr Plus.

Official Motorola Accessories: What's Available?

Motorola offers a variety of official accessories that pair perfectly with your Razr Plus, ensuring you get the best performance and functionality. These accessories include items like smartwatches, wireless headphones, chargers, cases, and more.

Here's a list of some of the most popular Motorola accessories:

1. **Motorola Smartwatches**:

    o **Moto 360 Smartwatch**: Offers fitness tracking, notifications, and more. It syncs seamlessly with your Razr Plus, making it easy to manage notifications, fitness goals, and calls directly from your wrist.

    o **Moto Watch 100**: A more affordable option, ideal for fitness enthusiasts.

Tracks your workouts, heart rate, and more.

2. **Wireless Headphones**:

   o **Moto Buds 600**: These wireless earbuds offer great sound quality and easy pairing with your Razr Plus. Perfect for listening to music or taking calls without the hassle of wires.

   o **Moto Pulse 2 Wireless Headphones**: For those who prefer over-ear headphones, these provide high-quality sound and comfort for extended wear.

3. **Motorola Cases and Accessories**:

   o **Moto Razr Plus Case**: Protects your device while adding a touch of style. Available in various designs like clear cases or wallet cases.

   o **Motorola Charging Pads**: Convenient wireless charging options for your Razr Plus to keep it powered up without plugging in cables.

4. **Motorola Docking Stations**:

   o **Moto Smart Dock**: Turns your phone into a desktop experience by connecting it to a larger screen. Perfect for those who need to multitask.

Using Wireless Headphones and Smartwatches with Razr Plus

Motorola's wireless headphones and smartwatches are designed to pair effortlessly with the Razr Plus. Let's go through how to connect and use them.

How to pair your wireless headphones with the Razr Plus:

1. **Turn on your wireless headphones**:

    o Make sure your headphones are charged and powered on.

    o Put them in pairing mode (this usually involves holding down the power button for a few seconds until you see a blinking light).

2. **Connect via Bluetooth**:

    o Open the **Settings** app on your Razr Plus.

    o Tap **Bluetooth** and make sure it's turned on.

    o Wait for your headphones to appear in the list of available devices.

    o Tap on the name of your headphones to pair them. Once paired, you'll hear a confirmation sound or see a notification on your screen.

How to pair a Motorola smartwatch with your Razr Plus:

1. **Turn on the smartwatch**:
   o Make sure your smartwatch is fully charged and powered on.

2. **Install the companion app**:
   o Download the **Moto Body** or **Moto Connect** app from the Google Play Store (depending on your smartwatch model).

   o Open the app and follow the on-screen instructions to connect your smartwatch via Bluetooth.

3. **Pair the devices**:
   o Once the app is installed, open it and it will prompt you to connect to your Motorola smartwatch. Follow the prompts to complete the pairing.

Tip: Once paired, you can manage notifications, control music, and even track your workouts directly from your smartwatch or headphones.

Motorola's Ready For: Connecting to TV and PC

Motorola's **Ready For** is an incredible feature that allows you to connect your Razr Plus to a larger screen like a TV or PC for a seamless experience. Whether you want to stream content, play mobile games on a big screen, or use your phone like a desktop computer, **Ready For** has you covered.

How to use Ready For to connect to a TV or PC:

1. **Connect your Razr Plus to the TV**:

    o   **Wireless Connection (via Wi-Fi)**:

        ▪   Ensure that both your Razr Plus
            and the TV are connected to the
            same Wi-Fi network.

        ▪   On your Razr Plus, swipe down
            to open the **Quick Settings
            menu**.

        ▪   Tap **Ready For** or **Cast**.

        ▪   Select your TV from the list of
            available devices.

        ▪   Your phone's screen will appear
            on your TV in seconds.

    o   **Wired Connection (via USB-C to
        HDMI)**:

        ▪   Plug a **USB-C to HDMI** adapter
            into your phone.

        ▪   Connect the HDMI end to your
            TV or monitor.

        ▪   Select the HDMI input on your
            TV.

        ▪   Your phone's screen will appear
            on the TV automatically.

2. **Use Ready For on your PC**:

    o   If you want to use Ready For on a PC,
        download and install the **Motorola**

Ready For app on your PC (available on select operating systems).

- o Follow the on-screen instructions to pair your phone and computer.

- o Once connected, you'll be able to use your Razr Plus like a desktop, accessing apps, transferring files, and more.

Tip: Ready For is great for video calls, presentations, or simply enjoying your media on a larger screen.

Setting Up Motorola's Smart Accessories

Motorola's smart accessories, such as the **Moto Smart Dock** or **Motorola smart headphones**, can elevate your experience. Here's how to set them up:

How to set up a Motorola Moto Smart Dock:

1. **Connect the dock to a monitor/TV**:

   - o Plug the dock into a monitor, TV, or computer via HDMI.

   - o Connect your Razr Plus to the dock using a USB-C cable.

2. **Launch Ready For**:

   - o Once connected, the **Ready For** screen should automatically appear on the connected display.

   - o You can now use your Razr Plus like a desktop. You can open apps, drag-and-drop files, or use your phone as a media hub.

Managing Software Updates for Accessories

Just like your phone, Motorola accessories such as smartwatches, headphones, and docks receive software updates to improve performance and add new features.

How to manage updates for your Motorola accessories:

1. **For Smartwatches**:

    o Open the **Moto Connect** or **Moto Body** app on your phone.

    o Go to **Settings** and tap **Device Info**.

    o If there's an update available for your smartwatch, you'll see an option to **Update**. Follow the on-screen instructions.

2. **For Headphones**:

    o Some Motorola wireless headphones will prompt you for updates through the **Motorola Connect** app.

    o If an update is available, simply follow the app's instructions to complete the update.

How to Trade In or Recycle Your Old Device

When upgrading to the Motorola Razr Plus, you may want to trade in your old device or recycle it. Motorola offers a convenient trade-in program.

How to trade in or recycle your old Motorola device:

1. **Visit Motorola's Trade-In Page**:

   o Go to Motorola's website and find the **Trade-In** section.

2. **Select Your Old Device**:

   o Enter the model and condition of your old device to get an estimate of its trade-in value.

3. **Send in Your Device**:

   o If you accept the trade-in offer, Motorola will send you a prepaid shipping label to send in your old device.

   o Once Motorola receives your device and verifies its condition, they'll send you a credit or payment, which can be used toward your new Razr Plus.

4. **Recycle Your Device**:

   o If you prefer to recycle your device instead of trading it in, Motorola also provides recycling options. Visit their recycling page for details on how to send in your old phone.

With Motorola's wide range of accessories, your Razr Plus can become even more powerful and versatile. Whether you're connecting to a TV, using a smartwatch for fitness tracking, or managing your accessories through the Ready For feature, you're able to seamlessly integrate Motorola's ecosystem into your everyday life. By following the steps in this chapter, you'll be able to maximize your phone's potential and enjoy a more connected experience.

Optimizing Your Razr Plus for Long-Term Use

Your Motorola Razr Plus is designed to last, but like any device, it requires a little care and attention to keep it running smoothly and looking great over the long haul. In this chapter, we'll walk you through some simple steps to ensure your Razr Plus stays in top condition, whether it's maintaining performance, protecting the foldable screen, or caring for the battery. Let's dive into the essential tips for keeping your phone in peak shape!

Regular Phone Maintenance: Cleaning and Updates

Why It's Important:

Regular maintenance is key to keeping your phone looking and functioning like new. With regular cleaning, system updates, and good habits, you can ensure that your Razr Plus continues to work at its best.

Cleaning Your Motorola Razr Plus:

Keeping your phone clean is one of the easiest ways to ensure it stays in great condition. Dust, fingerprints, and other debris can accumulate on your device over time, and if not cleaned regularly, they can impact both appearance and performance.

How to Clean Your Razr Plus:

- **Screen:** Use a microfiber cloth to gently wipe the screen. Avoid using paper towels or other rough materials that could scratch the screen.

- **Body:** Use a soft, lint-free cloth to clean the back and sides. Lightly dampen the cloth with water, but never apply liquid directly to the phone. Be careful around the ports and hinge area.

- **Charging Port and Ports:** Use a dry toothbrush or a compressed air canister to remove dirt or dust from the ports.

Software Updates:

Motorola regularly releases software updates that improve security, fix bugs, and sometimes add new features. Always keep your software up-to-date to ensure optimal performance and security.

- To check for updates, go to **Settings > System > Software Updates**. If an update is available, follow the on-screen instructions to install it.

Battery Care Tips: Ensuring Longevity

Why It's Important:

Battery health is crucial for long-term use. Over time, the battery's ability to hold a charge will naturally decrease, but there are a few practices you can adopt to slow down this process.

Best Practices for Battery Care:

- **Avoid Extreme Temperatures:** Exposing your phone to excessive heat or cold can damage the battery. Try to avoid leaving your phone in direct sunlight or in a cold car for long periods.

- **Don't Let Your Battery Drop Too Low:** Try not to let your phone's battery drop to 0% regularly. Charging it when it reaches around 20% to 30% is ideal.

- **Use the Right Charger:** Always use the charger that came with your Razr Plus or a certified compatible charger. Using cheap or low-quality chargers can harm the battery.

Battery Saver Mode:

If you find that your battery is draining quickly during the day, you can use Battery Saver mode. It disables background apps and reduces power consumption to extend battery life.

- To enable Battery Saver, go to **Settings > Battery > Battery Saver** and toggle it on.

When to Consider Upgrading Your Device

Why It's Important:

After years of use, you may notice that your Razr Plus is starting to show signs of aging, such as slower performance, a battery that doesn't last as long, or hardware issues. Knowing when it's time to upgrade can save you from frustration.

Signs It Might Be Time to Upgrade:

- **Battery Life Is Drastically Reduced:** If your battery no longer holds a charge for a full day, even with careful use, it may be time to consider a new phone.

- **Sluggish Performance:** If apps are slow to open, the phone freezes often, or multitasking becomes a challenge, it might be due to outdated hardware.

- **Broken or Worn-Out Screen:** If your foldable screen is damaged beyond repair or no longer functions properly, it may be worth upgrading.

Taking Care of the Foldable Screen: Best Practices

Why It's Important:

The foldable screen is one of the standout features of the Motorola Razr Plus. However, it's more delicate than a traditional screen, so taking care of it is essential to ensure it lasts.

How to Protect and Maintain the Foldable Screen:

- **Keep It Clean:** Wipe down the foldable screen regularly with a microfiber cloth. Be sure to avoid touching the screen with greasy or dirty hands.

- **Don't Overbend the Screen:** While the Razr Plus is designed to fold, it's still important not to force it. Always fold and unfold gently, and avoid doing so if there's any resistance.

- **Use a Screen Protector:** If you want extra protection, consider using a foldable screen protector designed specifically for the Razr Plus. This can help prevent scratches and other minor damage.

Preventing Wear and Tear on the Hinge

Why It's Important:

The hinge mechanism is one of the most crucial parts of the foldable phone. Regular use of the hinge can cause wear over time, but there are steps you can take to minimize this.

Tips for Maintaining the Hinge:

- **Keep It Clean:** Dust and debris can accumulate around the hinge, so it's important to keep it clean. Gently wipe the hinge area with a microfiber cloth to remove any particles that may cause friction.

- **Avoid Extreme Angles:** When folding the phone, don't force the hinge beyond its designed range of motion. This will prevent strain on the mechanism.

- **Be Gentle When Folding and Unfolding:** Always open and close the device with a smooth, gentle motion.

Monitoring System Performance Over Time

Why It's Important:

As time goes on, it's a good idea to keep an eye on how your Razr Plus is performing. If you notice any sudden drops in speed, performance, or battery life, it's worth troubleshooting before the issues worsen.

How to Monitor Performance:

- **Check Storage:** If your storage is almost full, it could slow down your phone. Go to **Settings > Storage** to see how much space is available. Delete any unneeded files or apps to free up space.

- **System Updates:** Make sure your phone's software is up-to-date. Motorola frequently releases updates to improve system performance.

- **App Management:** Review the apps you have installed and remove any that you no longer use. This will help free up system resources and keep the phone running smoothly.

By following these simple steps for maintaining and optimizing your Motorola Razr Plus, you'll be able to ensure that your phone stays in excellent condition for the long haul. Whether it's taking care of the battery, protecting the foldable screen, or keeping the hinge working smoothly, small regular actions can make a big difference in the lifespan of your device.

Remember, regular maintenance and careful use are the keys to keeping your Razr Plus performing at its best. Take these tips to heart, and you'll enjoy a smooth, reliable experience for years to come!

Eco-Friendly and Sustainability Features

Motorola has made a significant effort to integrate eco-friendly and sustainable practices into their products, and the Razr Plus is no exception. By choosing the Razr Plus, you're not only investing in cutting-edge technology but also supporting a company that values the environment. In this chapter, we'll walk you through Motorola's sustainability efforts and show you how you can play a role in reducing your environmental footprint while using your device.

Motorola's Commitment to Sustainability

Why It's Important:

Motorola understands that technology and sustainability go hand-in-hand. As a leading tech company, they are committed to reducing their environmental impact and creating products that are more sustainable, both in their manufacturing processes and their lifecycle.

Motorola's Sustainable Practices Include:

- **Energy Efficiency:** Motorola works on making its products energy-efficient to help conserve power throughout their use. This means that your Razr Plus is designed to optimize battery use and consumption.

- **Reducing Carbon Emissions:** By implementing eco-friendly manufacturing practices, Motorola has lowered the carbon emissions involved in producing the Razr Plus. This is part of a larger strategy to minimize environmental harm.

- **Recycling and Reuse:** Motorola encourages users to recycle their devices and packaging, promoting a circular economy. Many of the materials used in the Razr Plus, such as metals and plastics, are recyclable.

What You Can Do:

As a user, you can help by being mindful of how you use and dispose of your device. When it's time to upgrade, recycling your old device can help reduce waste and conserve resources.

Eco-Friendly Packaging and Materials

Why It's Important:

The environmental impact of products doesn't end with the device itself. Packaging is a significant contributor to waste. Motorola has made great strides in ensuring that its packaging is eco-friendly and sustainable.

What Makes the Razr Plus Packaging Eco-Friendly:

- **Recyclable Materials:** Motorola uses recyclable and sustainable materials for the packaging of the Razr Plus. This helps reduce the environmental impact by ensuring that packaging materials are reused or repurposed.

- **Minimalist Packaging:** To reduce waste, the packaging is designed to use as little material as necessary. This not only minimizes waste but also reduces the amount of energy required for production and shipping.

- **No Single-Use Plastics:** The packaging for the Razr Plus avoids single-use plastic components, which is a significant step towards reducing plastic waste in landfills and oceans.

What You Can Do:

- **Recycle the Packaging:** When you unpack your Razr Plus, make sure to recycle the cardboard, paper, and any other recyclable materials.

- **Avoid Waste:** Try to avoid excess packaging by reusing any boxes or materials for other purposes. This will help cut down on overall waste.

Recycling Your Motorola Razr Plus

Why It's Important:

As technology advances, older devices become outdated. Instead of throwing them away, Motorola encourages users to recycle their phones, ensuring that valuable materials like metals and plastics are reused and not wasted.

How to Recycle Your Motorola Razr Plus:

- **Trade-In Program:** Motorola offers a trade-in program where you can send in your old phone and receive credit toward a new device. This is a great way to ensure your old phone is reused responsibly.

- **Recycling Locations:** If you're not looking to trade in your device, you can take your old Razr Plus to an authorized recycling center. Many electronics stores and waste facilities accept old phones for recycling.

- **Recycling Instructions:** To prepare your device for recycling, make sure to remove all personal data from the phone. Perform a factory reset by going to **Settings > System > Reset**. This will erase all your data and prepare the phone for recycling.

Why It Matters:

Recycling old phones helps reduce e-waste, conserves natural resources, and keeps hazardous materials from harming the environment. By participating in these recycling efforts, you contribute to the global effort to reduce waste and preserve the planet.

Sustainable Device Usage Tips

Why It's Important:

There are several steps you can take during the everyday use of your Razr Plus to make sure you're using the device in an environmentally conscious way. Small changes in your habits can have a big impact over time.

Tips for Sustainable Usage:

1. **Battery Conservation:** Use energy-efficient features like **Battery Saver** to extend battery life and reduce the need for frequent charging. This will help conserve energy in the long run.

2. **Avoid Overcharging:** Avoid leaving your phone plugged in after it reaches 100%. Overcharging can contribute to wear on the battery, which could lead to more frequent replacements. It also uses unnecessary energy.

3. **Turn Off Unnecessary Features:** When you're not using Bluetooth, Wi-Fi, or GPS, turn them off to save battery and reduce energy consumption. This small action will help your phone run more efficiently.

4. **Update Regularly:** Keeping your phone's software updated helps optimize performance, which means the phone will last longer and operate more efficiently, helping you get the most out of your device.

Using Accessories Responsibly:

- Consider using accessories like **wireless headphones** and **smartwatches** that can also be recycled when they are no longer in use. Ensure they are properly disposed of by taking them to recycling centers.

Be Mindful of Device Longevity:

Instead of frequently upgrading your device, focus on maintaining your Razr Plus with regular care (as discussed in previous chapters). This helps reduce the demand for new resources and minimizes electronic waste.

By following these simple steps, you're not only caring for your Razr Plus but also contributing to a more sustainable future. Motorola has made it easy for you to engage in eco-friendly practices, from the recyclable packaging to the ability to trade in your old device. Whether it's using your phone efficiently, recycling, or upgrading responsibly, every small change counts toward a more sustainable planet.

Remember, every action you take in terms of sustainability, no matter how small, makes a difference. Thank you for doing your part!

Community and Support

No matter how much you enjoy using your Motorola Razr Plus, sometimes you may run into questions or need some assistance. Don't worry! Motorola has a variety of ways for you to get help. Whether you're troubleshooting an issue, looking for helpful tips, or need to request a repair, there's a community and support network available to assist you. Let's walk through the best ways to get the support you need.

Connecting with the Motorola Community

Why It's Important:

The Motorola community is made up of users like you, experts, and even Motorola staff who actively share their knowledge and experiences. Connecting with this community can be a great way to find answers to your questions, learn new tips, and interact with other Motorola Razr Plus users.

How to Connect:

- **Motorola Community Forums:**

  Visit the **Motorola Community Forums** to connect with other Razr Plus users. These forums are full of discussions about the latest updates, common issues, and tips from other users.

How to Join:

  o   Go to the Motorola website and navigate to the "Community" section.

- o Sign up for an account or log in if you already have one.

- o You can then start participating by asking questions or browsing through the threads.

- **Motorola Blogs:**

Check out **Motorola's official blog** for the latest news and tips. The blog covers everything from new updates, tips, tricks, and new features to community highlights. It's a great place to stay informed.

What You Can Do:

You can post questions, share your experience, or even offer solutions if you've figured something out. Engaging with the community allows you to learn from others and contribute to the ecosystem.

Joining Social Media Groups for Razr Plus Tips

Why It's Important:

Social media platforms have become a great way to connect with users and get real-time feedback and tips. Motorola's active presence on social media allows you to get up-to-date information, and joining groups focused on the Razr Plus can help you find solutions quickly.

Where to Connect:

- **Facebook Groups:**

Search for "Motorola Razr Plus" on Facebook to find user groups where you can ask questions and get answers. These groups often share user-generated content, helpful guides, and tips for solving problems.

- **Reddit:**
  On **Reddit**, there are subreddits like r/Motorola or r/Android where you can participate in discussions, share experiences, and ask questions.

- **Instagram & Twitter:**

  Motorola often shares new features, announcements, and tips on **Instagram** and **Twitter**. Following these accounts will keep you in the loop with any upcoming updates, sales, and troubleshooting tips.

What You Can Do:

Join these groups to learn from other users. Don't hesitate to post your own questions or insights. The social media community can often provide quick answers and helpful advice based on shared experiences.

Using Forums and Official Support Channels

Why It's Important:

Forums and official support channels are your go-to resources when you need help with more specific issues or official solutions. Whether it's a minor issue or a larger problem, these channels are designed to provide you with accurate information from Motorola's support team and fellow users.

Where to Get Help:

- **Motorola Official Support Website:**

  The **Motorola Support website** offers resources like FAQs, troubleshooting guides, and manuals. You can use this site to search for answers to common problems or get step-by-step instructions on fixing issues.

- **Motorola Community Forums (Detailed Support):**

  As mentioned earlier, the Motorola community forums are also a valuable place to get technical help, interact with other users, and access solutions shared by others.

What You Can Do:

If you can't find a solution on the forums or website, try the **live chat** feature, where you can directly talk to a Motorola support representative for more personalized help. You can also browse through detailed troubleshooting articles for specific problems.

Contacting Motorola Customer Service

Why It's Important:

If you need more personalized support or face an issue that requires immediate attention, contacting Motorola's customer service is the next best step. Their customer service team is trained to handle a wide range of problems, from technical issues to repair requests.

How to Contact:

- **Customer Support Number:**

  Call **Motorola's customer service hotline** for direct assistance. You can find the number on the official Motorola website under the "Contact Us" section. Make sure to have your Razr Plus's model and serial number ready to expedite the process.

- **Live Chat:**

  For quicker help, you can start a live chat with a support agent on the **Motorola support website**.

- **Email Support:**

  If you prefer email communication, you can send an email to Motorola's support team through their official contact page.

What You Can Do:

Prepare any relevant information before reaching out, like your device's model, software version, and a description of the issue. This helps the customer service team assist you more efficiently.

Requesting Repair or Warranty Service

Why It's Important:

If your Motorola Razr Plus is malfunctioning or has a hardware issue, you may need to send it in for repairs or request warranty service. Motorola offers warranty services that can cover repairs depending on the nature of the issue and the terms of your warranty.

Steps to Request Service:

- **Check Warranty Status:**

    Before requesting repairs, check your warranty status by visiting the **Motorola warranty page** and entering your device's serial number. This will tell you if your device is still under warranty.

- **Repair Request Process:**

    If your device needs repair, visit the **Motorola repair center website**. You'll need to follow their steps, which usually involve:

    o   Filling out an online form about the issue.

    o   Sending your device to their authorized repair center (Motorola will provide the address and shipping instructions).

- **Authorized Service Centers:**

    If you're unable to send your phone for repair, check for local **Motorola-authorized service centers** where you can visit in person for assistance.

What You Can Do:

If the issue is covered by your warranty, you can get your device repaired or replaced without any cost. Make sure to back up your data before sending it for repairs, as the device may be reset or replaced.

Whether you're dealing with technical issues, need help with a feature, or simply want to stay updated, Motorola provides many ways to get support. From connecting with the community to reaching out to customer service, you have several resources available to assist you. Don't hesitate to ask for help when you need it—Motorola's support system is designed to ensure that your Razr Plus experience is as smooth as possible.

Glossary and Technical Terms

Glossary of Common Smartphone Terms

This section provides an easy-to-understand explanation of key terms that you may come across while using your Motorola Razr Plus or exploring its features.

- **Android OS**: The operating system used by the Razr Plus and many other smartphones. It's the software that makes your phone work, allowing you to run apps, manage settings, and use all its features.

- **App**: Short for "application." Apps are programs you download to your phone to perform different tasks, such as messaging, social media, music, etc.

- **Battery Health**: Refers to the overall condition and longevity of your phone's battery. Maintaining good battery health helps ensure the phone runs efficiently over time.

- **Bluetooth**: A wireless technology that allows your phone to connect to nearby devices like headphones, speakers, and car systems.

- **Cache**: Temporary files that your phone stores to make apps run faster. Sometimes, clearing the cache can help with performance issues.

- **Cloud Storage**: A way to save files, photos, and videos on the internet, instead of storing them directly on your phone. Examples include Google Drive and iCloud.

- **Data Encryption**: The process of converting information into a secure format, ensuring that your data is safe from unauthorized access.

- **Firmware**: The software that is embedded in your phone's hardware. It controls how the phone operates and is periodically updated to improve performance or add new features.

Understanding Foldable Phone Terminology

Since the Motorola Razr Plus is a foldable phone, here are some important terms to help you understand its design and functionality:

- **Foldable Display**: A type of screen that bends without breaking, allowing the phone to fold in half. This is a standout feature of the Razr Plus, making it compact and portable.

- **Flex Mode**: A feature of foldable phones where the screen automatically adjusts when the device is partially folded, allowing you to use the top and bottom halves of the screen for different tasks.

- **Hinge Mechanism**: The hardware inside the phone that allows it to fold. It's carefully designed for durability and smooth operation.

- **Crease**: The visible line that runs down the middle of a foldable screen, where it bends. It's a normal part of foldable displays, but it's important to take care to avoid excessive pressure on this area.

- **Unfolded Mode**: The phone's fully extended display, which allows you to use the entire screen without interruption.

Key Features in Android 14 Explained

Android 14 brings new features and improvements to enhance your experience with the Razr Plus. Here are some key terms and features to help you navigate the operating system:

- **Android 14**: The latest version of the Android operating system, which includes performance enhancements, privacy features, and new capabilities for foldable screens.

- **App Permissions**: Settings that control what apps can access on your phone, like your location or camera. Android 14 has improved controls to ensure privacy.

- **Battery Optimization**: Tools in Android 14 that help extend battery life by limiting background processes and apps that consume power.

- **Gestures**: Actions you can perform on the screen, such as swiping or tapping, that replace buttons for navigating your phone. Android 14 includes more gesture options for quicker navigation.

- **Multitasking**: The ability to run multiple apps at once. On foldable phones, Android 14 allows for more dynamic multitasking, with features like split-screen and floating windows.

- **Picture-in-Picture (PiP)**: A feature that allows you to watch a video in a small window while using other apps. It's particularly useful for multitasking and makes it easier to use your phone while watching content.

- **Security and Privacy Controls**: In Android 14, these settings give you more control over your personal data. You can manage app access, location settings, and more to ensure that your information stays safe.

- **Themes**: Android 14 allows you to customize the look and feel of your phone with dark mode, custom icons, and a variety of theme options.

Real-Life Examples for Context

To make these terms more relatable, let's consider a few scenarios:

1. **Bluetooth Example**: When you connect your wireless headphones to the Razr Plus, you're using Bluetooth. Once connected, you can listen to music, take calls, or even control your phone's audio without needing to plug anything in.

2. **Cache Management Example**: If you notice that your apps are running slowly, it may be due to a buildup of cached data. By clearing your cache, you free up space and improve your phone's performance, just like cleaning up a cluttered desk.

3. **Battery Health Example**: Imagine you've had your Razr Plus for a while and notice it's charging slower than before. Checking your battery health can tell you if the battery needs replacing, helping you make informed decisions about its future use.

4. **Picture-in-Picture (PiP) Example**: If you're watching a YouTube video and want to respond to a message at the same time, PiP mode allows you to keep the video playing in a small window while you chat in the background.

5. **Gestures Example**: Instead of pressing buttons, Android 14 allows you to swipe up or swipe from the edges of the screen to navigate your phone. This can speed up your workflow, especially when multitasking or switching between apps.

This glossary provides you with the tools to understand and navigate the Motorola Razr Plus and Android 14 more easily. By learning these key terms, you'll be able to make the most of your phone, ensuring a smoother and more efficient experience. If you encounter new features or terms in the future, refer back to this glossary for a quick explanation!

Appendices

Welcome to the **Appendices** section! Here you'll find all the extra resources that can help you troubleshoot common issues, understand your device better, and find the support you need. This section includes quick reference guides, frequently asked questions, product support details, and more to ensure you're always equipped to make the most of your Motorola Razr Plus.

Quick Reference Charts

This chart provides a quick overview of essential features and settings you might need in a pinch. Keep it handy for when you're in a hurry!

Feature	Where to Find It	Description
Wi-Fi Settings	Settings > Network & Internet > Wi-Fi	Connect to and manage your Wi-Fi networks.
Battery Saver Mode	Settings > Battery > Battery Saver	Extend battery life by limiting background apps.
Bluetooth	Settings > Connected Devices > Bluetooth	Pair your device with wireless devices like headphones.
Screen Brightness	Settings > Display > Brightness	Adjust how bright or dim your screen is.

Feature	Where to Find It	Description
App Permissions	Settings > Apps & Notifications > Permissions	Manage which apps can access your data.

Frequently Asked Questions (FAQ)

Here are answers to some of the most common questions we get about the Motorola Razr Plus:

1. **How do I take a screenshot?**

   o Press the **Volume Down** button and the **Power** button simultaneously for a couple of seconds. The screen will flash to indicate that the screenshot has been captured.

2. **How can I free up storage space?**

   o Go to **Settings > Storage**, and you can review your data. Delete unnecessary files, clear app caches, or move files to Google Drive or an SD card.

3. **What do I do if my phone isn't charging properly?**

   o First, try a different charger or cable to rule out hardware issues. If the problem persists, restart your phone and check the charging port for any debris. If it still doesn't work, consider contacting customer support.

4. **How do I enable dark mode?**

- Go to **Settings > Display > Dark theme**, and toggle the switch to turn on dark mode for a more comfortable, eye-friendly experience.

5. **How do I reset my phone to factory settings?**

- Go to **Settings > System > Reset options > Erase all data**. This will erase all your data, so be sure to back up your important files first.

Troubleshooting Index

Having trouble? Here are some quick fixes for the most common issues with your Motorola Razr Plus:

1. **My screen is not responding**:

- Ensure the screen is clean and free of debris. If the issue persists, restart the phone or perform a soft reset by holding the **Power** button for 10-20 seconds.

2. **Wi-Fi is not connecting**:

- Make sure your Wi-Fi is enabled and try restarting both your phone and the router. If it still doesn't work, forget the network and reconnect by entering the password again.

3. **My battery is draining too quickly**:

- Check for apps that are using excessive battery by going to **Settings > Battery > Battery Usage**. You can enable **Battery**

Saver or restrict background apps to conserve power.

4. **My phone is overheating**:

    o Overheating can happen if you're running multiple apps at once or using heavy apps (like games). Close any unused apps and allow your phone to cool down before using it again.

5. **My apps are crashing**:

    o Try clearing the app's cache by going to **Settings > Apps & notifications > See all apps > [App Name] > Storage & cache** and tap **Clear cache**. If the issue persists, reinstall the app.

Product Support Links

While we don't include direct links, here's how you can find the support you need:

- **Customer Service**: Visit the official Motorola website to find phone numbers, email addresses, or chat support options to contact customer service for any technical assistance or inquiries.

- **Online Forums**: Join online communities and forums where Motorola users discuss common issues and solutions. You can find tips from other Razr Plus users or post your own questions.

- **Repair Services**: If your phone requires physical repair, check the Motorola website for service centers near you or inquire about sending your device in for repair.

Glossary of Terms

We've included a glossary of important terms you might encounter in this manual. Refer to **Chapter 18: Glossary and Technical Terms** for a deeper dive into smartphone jargon, but here are a few basics:

- **ROM**: The phone's internal memory, which stores the operating system and all your apps.

- **RAM**: Temporary memory that your phone uses to run apps smoothly.

- **OTA Update**: Over-the-air updates sent by the manufacturer to improve your phone's performance or add new features.

- **USB-C**: The standard charging and data transfer port for your Motorola Razr Plus.

Motorola Product Warranty and Return Policy

Motorola provides a standard warranty for all devices that covers defects in materials and workmanship. The warranty typically lasts for one year from the date of purchase. You can return or exchange your device if it's within the return window specified by Motorola. Be sure to keep your purchase receipt or proof of purchase, as you will need this for warranty claims or returns.

For detailed information on the warranty terms, you can visit Motorola's official customer service pages or reach out to their support team.

Links to Motorola's Official Video Tutorials

Motorola offers a variety of video tutorials that provide in-depth guides on how to use your Razr Plus. These videos cover everything from basic setup to advanced features like using the foldable screen or optimizing performance for gaming. To access these tutorials, simply visit Motorola's official YouTube channel or support section on their website.

By keeping these appendices in mind, you'll have quick access to all the essential resources to troubleshoot issues, understand important terms, and make the most of your Motorola Razr Plus. If you have any questions, don't hesitate to reach out to Motorola's customer support for further help!

Conclusion

Congratulations on reaching the end of this comprehensive guide to using your Motorola Razr Plus! We hope that this manual has equipped you with the knowledge and confidence to make the most of your device, whether you're just starting out or you're diving into more advanced features.

Throughout this guide, we've covered everything from the basic setup and customization to advanced features and troubleshooting, all with the goal of helping you get the best experience with your phone. Remember, the Razr Plus isn't just a device — it's a tool to enhance your productivity, entertainment, and lifestyle.

Take the time to explore, experiment, and discover what works best for you. The world of Android and Motorola is vast, and your phone has so much to offer — from the foldable screen to unique features like Moto Voice and Ready For mode. With this guide, you should now feel empowered to unlock the full potential of your Motorola Razr Plus.

Thank you for trusting us with your journey through the Motorola Razr Plus experience. If you ever encounter any issues, remember there are numerous resources available — from official support to online communities — that can assist you.

We wish you a seamless and enjoyable experience with your Motorola Razr Plus. Happy exploring!